Internet Research

SECOND EDITION-ILLUSTRATED

Internet Research

SECOND EDITION–ILLUSTRATED

Donald I. Barker
Carol D. Terry

THOMSON
COURSE TECHNOLOGY

Australia • Canada • Mexico • Singapore • Spain • United Kingdom • United States

Internet Research, Second Edition - Illustrated

Donald I. Barker, Carol D. Terry

Executive Editor: Nicole Jones Pinard	**Product Manager:** Christina Kling Garrett	**Associate Product Manager:** Emilie Perreault
Production Editor: Catherine G. DiMassa	**Developmental Editor:** Kim Crowley	**Editorial Assistant:** Shana Rosenthal
QA Manuscript Reviewers: Danielle Shaw, Burt LaFontaine	**Text Designer:** Joseph Lee, Black Fish Design	**Composition House:** GEX Publishing Services

ISBN 0-619-27325-9

The Illustrated Series Vision

Teaching and writing about computer applications and information literacy can be extremely challenging but rewarding. How do we engage students and keep their interest? How do we teach them skills that they can easily apply on the job? As we set out to write this book, our goals were to develop a textbook that:

- works for a beginning student

- provides varied, flexible, and meaningful exercises and projects to reinforce the skills

- serves as a reference tool

- makes your job as an educator easier, by providing a variety of supplementary resources to help you teach your course

Our popular, streamlined format is based on feedback we've received over the years from instructional designers and customers. This flexible design presents each lesson on a two-page spread, with step-by-step instructions on the left, and screen illustrations on the right. This signature style, coupled with high-caliber content, provides a comprehensive introduction to the crucial skills of conducting Internet research and a rich learning experience for the student.

Acknowledgments

Creating a book is a team effort. We would like to thank: our spouses, Chia-Ling Barker and Paul Turner, for their unfailing patience and generous support; Nicole Pinard for publishing the book; Christina Kling Garrett for managing the project; and our excellent developmental editor, Kim Crowley, for corrections and invaluable suggestions.
Donald I. Barker and Carol D. Terry

Preface

Welcome to *Internet Research, Second Edition–Illustrated*. Each lesson in the book contains elements pictured to the right in the sample two-page spread.

How is the book organized?

The book is organized into four units on conducting effective Internet research, from conducting basic searches with search engines using keywords and phrases, to creating complex searches using Boolean logic. Subject guides and specialized tools are also covered, including periodical databases, government resources, online reference sources, mailing lists, newsgroups, and intelligent search agents.

What kinds of assignments are included in the book? At what level of difficulty?

The lesson assignments use the interesting and relevant case study of alternative energy. As part of the city planning office in Portland, Oregon, you conduct research on different energy resources that will help the city to become "energy independent." The assignments are found on the light purple pages at the end of each unit and they progressively increase in difficulty. Assignments include:

- **Concepts Reviews** to test your knowledge with multiple choice, matching, and screen identification questions.

- **Skills Reviews** to provide additional hands-on, step-by-step reinforcement.

- **Independent Challenges** that are case projects requiring critical thinking and application of the skills learned in the unit. The Independent Challenges increase in difficulty, with the first Independent Challenge in each unit being the easiest (with the most step-by-step, detailed instructions).

Each 2-page spread focuses on a single skill.

Concise text that introduces the basic principles in the lesson and integrates the brief case study (indicated by the paintbrush icon).

UNIT B
Internet Research

Searching with Filters

Another way to refine a search is to use filters. **Filters** are programs that tell search tools to screen out specified types of Web pages or files. They are usually located on Advanced Search pages. As you develop your search strategy, use filters to search only a specified area of the Web or to exclude specified areas of the Web. For example, you use language filters to search only for pages in English, or date filters to search only for pages updated in the last year, or for certain file types like images, audio, or video. Table B-4 lists examples of filter options available on Google's Advanced Search page. Your colleague at the Portland City Planning Office tells you that Denmark is a leader in wind power. You would like to see some Danish sites, but because you don't read Danish, you need to find pages that are in English. Jane suggests you use filters to focus the search. To use filters, you go to an Advanced Search page.

STEPS

1. **At the Google site, click** Advanced Search
   The Google Advanced Search page appears displaying the Google filter options. Google also provides special filter options for searching images and groups on the Advanced Image Search page and Advanced Groups Search page.

2. **Click the** Language list box, **then click** English
   English should be selected, as shown in Figure B-11. With this filter selected, your search results will only include Web pages written in English. Now you want to restrict your search to the domain exclusive to Denmark. You searched earlier and found that .dk is the domain for Demark.

QUICK TIP
The Domains filter lets you choose between "Only return results from the site or domain" or "Don't return results from the site or domain." In this search, you want it to read Only.

3. **Type** .dk **in the Domains filter text box**
   The Domains text box should appear as shown in Figure B-11. With this filter selected, your search results will only include Web pages from Denmark.

4. **Type** wind power **in the** with the exact phrase text box **then click the** Google Search button
   Quotation marks are not needed to indicate a phrase search. This specialized text box interprets any words typed into it as a phrase, so quotation marks are assumed. Figure B-12 illustrates the results in a Venn diagram. The Web pages returned contain the phrase *wind power*, are in English, and are from Denmark's domain.

5. **Use the Lesson 6 table in the Data File to record the number of search results, then save the Data File**
   Note that Google has translated your search as "*wind power" site:.dk*. Quotation marks show how Google interpreted the words you typed into the "with the exact phrase" box. The *site:.dk* is how Google translated your domain filter selection. Just below the tabs you see that Google searched only pages in English. Google reiterates your query as Searched *English* pages for "*wind power" site:.dk*. Check this information to determine if the filters worked the way you expected when you developed the search strategy.

TABLE B-4: Examples of filters at Google's Advanced Search page

Language	Limits search to pages written in the language you choose (English, French, Japanese, etc.)
File Format	Limits search to pages in the format you choose (.pdf, .xls, .doc, etc.)
Date	Limits search to pages updated within a specified time period (3, 6, or 12 months)
Occurrences	Limits search to pages containing your keywords in the location you choose (URL, title, links, etc.)
Domain	Limits search to include pages only with a specified domain or to exclude pages with a specified domain
Safe Search	Limits search by filtering to exclude potentially offensive pages (can be hit and miss)

32 UNIT B: CONSTRUCTING COMPLEX SEARCHES

Hints as well as troubleshooting advice, right where you need it – next to the step itself.

Quickly accessible summaries of key terms, toolbar buttons, or keyboard alternatives connected with the lesson material. Students can refer easily to this information when working on their own projects at a later time.

Every lesson features large, full-color representations of what the screen should look like as students complete the numbered steps.

FIGURE B-11: Boolean logic and filters on Google's Advanced Search page

FIGURE B-12: Venn diagram for: "wind power" domain:.dk language: English

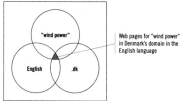

Web pages for "wind power" in Denmark's domain in the English language

Clues to Use boxes provide concise information that either expands on the major lesson skill or describes an independent task that in some way relates to the major lesson skill.

Subsequent Independent Challenges become increasingly open-ended, requiring more independent thinking and problem solving.

- **Advanced Challenge Exercises** set within the Independent Challenges provide optional tasks for more advanced students.

- **Visual Workshops** are practical, self-graded capstone projects that require independent problem solving.

What Web resources supplement the book?

Internet Research–Illustrated, Second Edition features a Student Online Companion (SOC) Web site. Use the SOC to access all the links referenced in the book, and to access other resources for further information. Since the Internet and search engines change frequently, the SOC will also contain any updates or clarifications to the text after its publication.

Clues to Use

Filtering domains in the URL

Filters search only for letters or words that appear in certain parts of a URL. The final two or three letters in the URL indicate domains. Web sites in the United States have URLs that end in three letters that represent the type of organization hosting the Web site. For example: university sites end in .edu; government sites end in .gov; commercial sites end in .com; and nonprofits end in .org. Others include: .biz, .pro, .info, .net, .us, .coop, .museum, and .name. Web sites located in other countries use 2-letter country codes: Canada's domain is .ca; the United Kingdom's domain is .uk; Japan's domain is .jp. Any of these 2- or 3-letter codes can limit search results when using a domain filter. For a full listing of the 2-letter country codes, go to www.iana.org/cctld/cctld-whois.htm. You can find other sites with this information by searching for: *countries* AND *domains*.

UNIT B: CONSTRUCTING COMPLEX SEARCHES **33**

Internet Research

Instructor Resources

The Instructor Resources CD puts the resources and information needed to teach and learn effectively directly into your hands. This integrated array of teaching and learning tools offers you and your students a broad range of technology-based instructional options, and we believe this CD represents the highest quality, most cutting edge resources available to instructors today. Many of the components are available at www.course.com. The resources available with this book are:

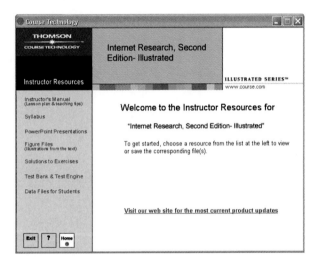

Instructor's Manual-Available as an electronic file, the Instructor's Manual is quality-assurance tested and includes unit overviews and detailed lecture topics with teaching tips for each unit.

Sample Syllabus-Prepare and customize our course easily using this sample course outline.

PowerPoint Presentations-Each unit has a corresponding PowerPoint Presentation that you can use in lecture, distribute to your students, or customize to suit your course.

Figure Files-The figures in the text are provided on the Instructor Resources CD to help you illustrate key topics or concepts. You can create traditional overhead transparencies by printing the figure files. Or you can create electronic slide shows by using the figures in a presentation program such as PowerPoint.

Solutions to Exercises-Solutions to Exercises contain every file students are asked to create or modify in the lessons and End-of-Unit material. A Help file on the Instructor Resources CD includes information for

using the Solution Files. There is also a document outlining the solutions for the End-of-Unit Concepts Review, Skills Review, and Independent Challenges.

ExamView Test Bank and Test Engine-ExamView is a powerful testing software package that allows you to create and administer printer, computer (LAN-based), and Internet exams. ExamView includes hundreds of questions that correspond to the topics covered in this text, enabling students to generate detailed study guides that include page references for further review. The computer-based and Internet testing components allow students to take exams at their computers, and also saves you time by grading each exam automatically.

Data Files for Students-To complete most of the units in this book, your students will need **Data Files**. Put them on a file server for students to copy. The Data Files are available on the Instructor Resources CD-ROM, the Review Pack, and can also be downloaded from www.course.com

Brief Contents

Contents

Read This Before You Begin

Are there any prerequisites for this book?

This book focuses on using the Internet effectively as a powerful research tool. It assumes that you are familiar with the Internet and Internet terms, and know basic Web-browsing skills. Basic Web-browsing skills include using the menus and toolbars in the browser of your choice, entering URLs, and navigating the Web using hyperlinks. In order to complete the exercises using the Data Files, you should also have basic word-processing skills.

What software do I need in order to use this book?

You will need an Internet connection, a Web browser, and a text-editing or word-processing program such as Microsoft Word or WordPad, in order to complete the lessons and exercises in this book. You can be running any recent version of the Windows operating system after and including Windows 95, Linux, and the Mac operating systems. This book was written and tested using Microsoft Internet Explorer 6 and Microsoft Windows XP. If you are working with a different browser or in a different operating system, your screens might look slightly different from those shown in the book. Data Files have been verified in these environments.

What are Data Files and how do I use them?

Data Files are text files in Microsoft Word format that you use to answer questions about your research results. You use a Data File in most lessons and in some of the exercises. Typically, you open the designated file and save it with a new name.

What is the Student Online Companion and how do I use it?

You use the Student Online Companion (SOC), located at www.course.com/illustrated/research2, to access all the links used in the book. Because the Internet and its search engines change frequently, the SOC will provide updates to the text as necessary. To access the SOC quickly, add the SOC URL to your Favorites or Bookmarks, or set it as your home page. (If you are working in a lab, please ask your instructor before doing this.) The URL is provided throughout the book in steps and tips for easy reference as well.

Credits

Figures A-7, A-8: AOL screenshots © 2004 America Online, Inc. Used with permission.
Figures A-10, A-11, A-12, A-13, A-17: Google. Google™ is a trademark of Google Inc.
Figure A-16: Courtesy of HowStuffWorks.com
Figure A-18: Reproduced with permission from the Library and Archives Canada's Web site, www.collectionscanada.ca/hockey
Figures B-3, B-5, B-7, B-11, B-13: Google search engine. Google™ is a trademark of Google Inc.
Figure B-14: Courtesy of IxQuick (www.IxQuick.com).
Figure B-19: Courtesy of the Charles W. Stockey Centre for the Performing Arts and the Bobby Orr Hall of Fame.
Figure C-5: Courtesy of LookSmart, Ltd.
Figure C-6: Courtesy of The Open Directory Project (www.dmoz.org).
Figures C-7, C-8, C-9: Courtesy of BUBL Information Service.
Figures C-13, C-14, C-15: Courtesy of Momentum Technologies LLC.
Figure C-17: Courtesy of the Florida Solar Energy Center; Hydrogen Research and Applications Center.
Figures C-18, C-19: Courtesy of Virginia Polytechnic Institute and State University.
Figure C-20: Courtesy of Dr. John K. Costain.
Figures D-2, D-3: Reproduced with permission of Yahoo! Inc. 2004 by Yahoo! Inc. YAHOO! and the YAHOO! logo are trademarks of Yahoo! Inc.
Figure D-4: Courtesy of InfoSpace, Inc.
Figures D-5, D-6, D-7: Courtesy of Switchboard Incorporated © 2004 (www.switchboard.com). All rights reserved.
Figure D-9: Courtesy of Hot Neuron LLC.
Figures D-12, D-13: Reproduced with permission of the Regents of the University of Michigan.
Figures D-15, D-18: Google Groups™ is a trademark of Google Inc.
Figures D-16, D-17: Courtesy of Intelliseek, Inc.

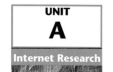

Searching the Internet Effectively

OBJECTIVES

Understand Internet search tools
Create an Internet research strategy
Identify the right keywords
Perform a basic search
Use phrases
Analyze search results
Cite online resources

The **World Wide Web** is an enormous repository of information stored on millions of computers all over the world. The **Internet** is a vast global network of interconnected networks that allows you to find and connect to information on the Web. Finding information on the Web is deceptively easy. In fact, finding lots of information is easier than finding the right information. In this unit you will learn about types of Internet search tools, how to develop a search strategy to transform your initial question into an effective **search query**, how to perform basic searches, how to analyze your search results, and how to use a standardized format to cite Web pages. You work in the City Planning Office in Portland, Oregon. A proposition has recently passed that mandates the city work toward becoming energy independent in the near future. You are working with a team to create a list of useful Web resources. Your area of responsibility is to identify Web pages related to alternative energy. Although you have surfed the Web, you realize your skills need some polishing to do a quality job with this important assignment. You have a friend, Jane Brodkin, who is a librarian at the Portland Public Library, and you ask her to help you learn the basics of Internet searching.

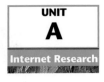

UNIT A

Internet Research

Understanding Internet Search Tools

Internet search tools are services which help you locate information on the Web and the Internet. Search tools can be divided into four major categories: search engines, metasearch engines, subject guides, and specialized search tools. Different search tools are better for finding different types of information, and no tool searches the entire Internet. Figure A-1 illustrates the four types of search tools and the main areas of the Internet and Web that these different search tools reach. (This figure does not represent to what depth these tools actually penetrate the Internet and the Web—that would be truly difficult to graphically represent.) ▄▄▟▛▜ Before you start your search for Web pages about alternative energy, Jane gives you a brief overview of the different search tools.

DETAILS

Types of search tools include:

QUICK TIP

To find out more about search engines, click the Search Engine Watch or Search Engine Showdown link on the Student Online Companion, at www.course.com/illustrated/research2.

- **Search engines** enable you to locate Web pages that contain keywords you enter in a search form. **Keywords** are the nouns and verbs, and sometimes important adjectives, which describe the major concepts of your search topic. A program called a **spider** crawls (scans) the Web to index the keywords in Web pages. The indexes, or indices, created by spiders match the keywords you enter in a search engine and return a list of links to Web pages that contain these keywords. Because this is a precise process, it provides a narrow search of the Web and works well for finding specific content. Because spiders take months to index even a small portion of the Web, search engine results are limited and some may be out of date. No single search engine covers the entire Web, so consider using more than one engine for important searches.

- **Metasearch engines** offer a single search form to query multiple search engines simultaneously. As with search engines, you enter keywords to retrieve links to Web pages that contain matching information. Search results are compiled from other search engines, rather than the Web. Metasearches are useful for quickly providing the highest ranked results from multiple search engines. Better metasearch engines remove duplicate results and rank the results based on relevancy to your query. Unfortunately, these results are not optimum. The best search engines are usually excluded from a metasearch because they charge fees and metasearch engine providers decline to pay them.

- **Subject guides** offer hierarchically organized topical directories which you navigate through to find relevant links. This design makes subject guides a good choice for a broad view of a topic. Subject guides are typically prepared by hand and vary in selectivity, criteria for inclusion, qualifications of human indexers, and levels of maintenance. Some are professional or academic sponsored, while others are commercial. Better subject guides also provide keyword searches of their database.

QUICK TIP

Major search engines are constantly working toward being able to search parts of the Web that are now invisible to their spiders.

- **Specialized search tools** allow you to find information that is "invisible" to traditional search engines or subject guides. The vast majority of the information on the Web is in this invisible area, usually called the **deep Web**. This information is stored in proprietary databases or in specialty directories, reference sites, and newsgroups. To retrieve this information, you must go to a specific site and use its unique search interface. Although many of these sites require **subscriptions** or fees for access, some can be searched with a relatively new breed of software, called **intelligent search agents**, which can query multiple specialty sites and/or search engines simultaneously. Intelligent search agents can actually search more of the Internet than conventional search tools such as search engines and subject guides.

FIGURE A-1: Internet search tools

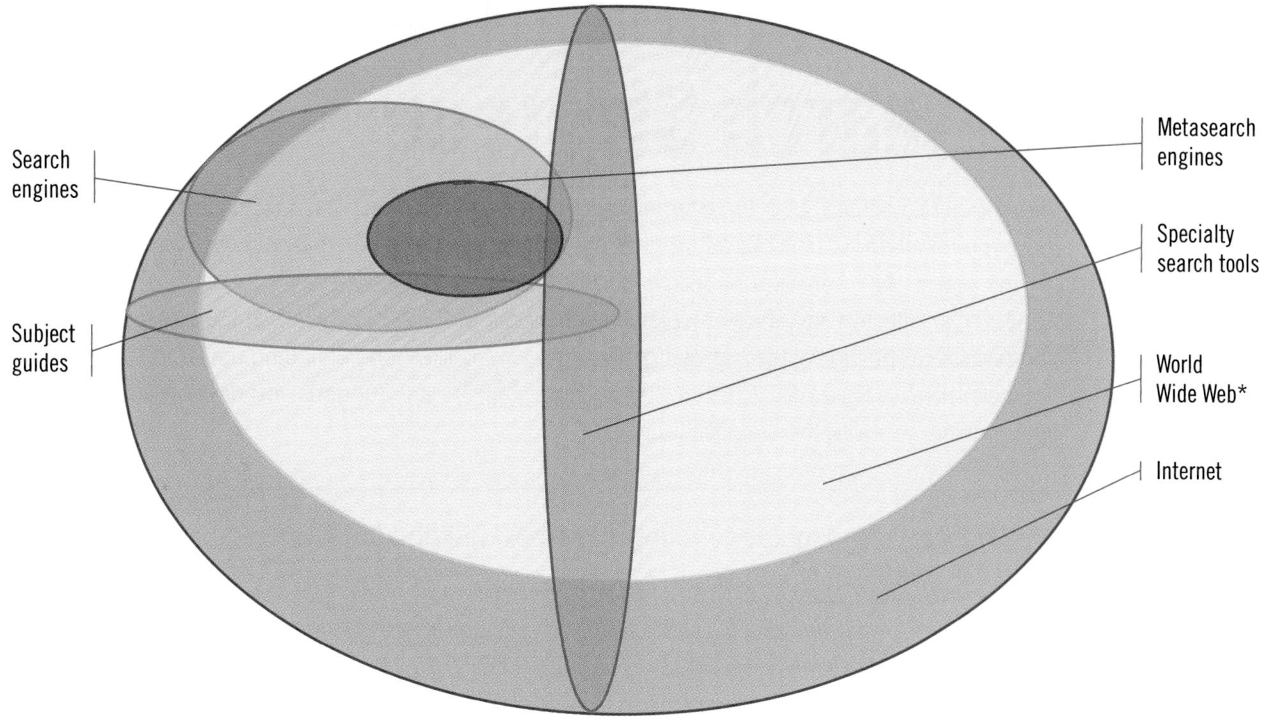

Search engines

Subject guides

Metasearch engines

Specialty search tools

World Wide Web*

Internet

*The part of the Web that is searched by search engines or subject guides represents the "visible" or "surface Web." The part of the **Web** that is not covered by **search engines** or **subject guides** represents the "invisible" or "deep Web." Some of the information in this area is accessible via **specialty search tools**. However, the areas representing the unsearched deep Web and the Internet are larger than they appear above. It has been estimated that the deep Web is 500 times the area of the visible Web.

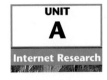
Creating an Internet Research Strategy

Before you begin a search on the Internet, you first need to focus on what information you want to find and how you might find it. The biggest mistake made by inexperienced searchers is entering only one keyword in any search tool. This kind of search usually produces an overwhelming list of mostly useless results. However, an effective and efficient research strategy can produce mostly relevant, useful results. The following seven steps provide guidelines that greatly increase the likelihood of finding the information you need in a timely manner. Figure A-2 illustrates these steps. Jane suggests you develop a research strategy and provides you with these guidelines.

DETAILS

Use Figure A-2 as a guide to follow the steps described below:

- **Define your topic and note initial keywords**
  Ask yourself what you want to end up with when you finish your research. Write down your topic. Note keywords and phrases. You don't have to use complete sentences, but be thorough in identifying concepts.

QUICK TIP

If you get stuck at any point in your research, consult your local reference librarians. They are information experts.

- **Locate background information and identify additional keywords**
  If you initially know very little about the topic you are researching, look for general information in encyclopedias, periodicals, and reference sources first. They can give you a good foundation for your research and provide keywords to use in your search. When you come across potentially useful keywords, note them and their correct spellings so you can use them in your search query.

- **Choose the proper search tool**
  If the Web is a good place to look for your topic, you need to decide where to look. Use the search tools that are best suited to retrieving the type of information you want to find. Table A-1 lists the most common search tools and provides information on how to select the best tool for your research needs. If you want specific content, then search engines or metasearch engines are appropriate. For a broader view, or when you know less about your topic, use subject guides. When seeking information not normally tracked by these tools, turn to specialty search tools. Combining these search tools will provide the most thorough approach.

- **Translate your question into an effective search query**
  The first step in translating a question into an effective **search query**—which consists of a word, words, phrases, and symbols that a search engine can interpret—is to identify the keywords that best describe the topic. You use keywords to query either search engines or multiple search engines in a metasearch engine. You also use keywords to construct complex searches for even more accuracy.

- **Perform your search**
  Search engines offer a variety of different **search forms**, which contain fields in which you enter information specific to your search. Although some subject guides allow keyword searches, they are usually searched by clicking a series of links to reach the information you seek. In either case, the information you provide is used to return search results. Search results are the Web pages the search tool returns to you in response to your search query.

- **Evaluate your search results**
  The quantity and quality of results vary from one search engine to another. To ascertain the value of the information you find, you need to apply **evaluative criteria**, such as who authored the Web page or how current the information is.

- **Refine your search, if needed**
  You may need to go back to a previous step in the research process to refine your strategy if the quality or quantity of results is not what you need. Use what you learned from your first pass through this process to refine your search. First, try fine-tuning your search query, and then try a different search tool. If you are still not satisfied with your results, you may need to reevaluate your keywords. Perhaps they are too specific or obscure. If you are unable to do this or it isn't successful, you may need to seek more basic information on your topic. Or, rethink the topic—you may find that redefining it, based on what you have seen in your searches, might be helpful.

FIGURE A-2: Developing a research strategy

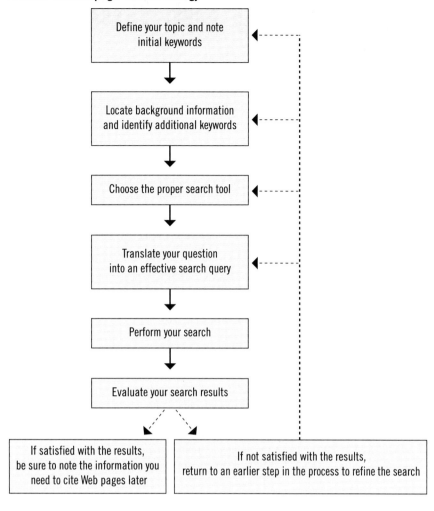

TABLE A-1: Common search tools

search tool	best for	where it searches	how to search	example information	example tools
Search engines	General or specific	Searches its own indexes that are compiled from data gathered from the Web	Enter keywords, phrases, or complex searches	Alternative energy or solar panels	Google, AltaVista
Metasearch engines	General or specific	Searches the indexes of multiple search engines simultaneously	Enter keywords, phrases, or complex searches	Alternative energy or solar panels	Ixquick, Vivisimo
Subject guides	More general	Searches its own files or database	Click through subject categories (may allow keyword searches)	Alternative energy	lii.org, WWW Virtual Library
Specialized tools	More specific	Searches "invisible" databases, directories, reference sites, and newsgroups	Enter keywords, phrases, or complex searches	Latest news on solar panels	ProFusion, The Source for Renewable Energy

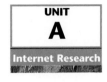

Identifying the Right Keywords

Once you have identified your research topic, you need to translate it into a search strategy that optimizes your chances of finding useful information. The main elements in your search strategy are the keywords that describe the major concepts of your search topic. It is these keywords that you enter into the search tool and which the search tool uses to return results. ▟▟▟▟▟ Jane directs you to use the guidelines below in creating a list of keywords to use in the search for Web resources on alternative energy.

DETAILS

Follow these guidelines to create a list of keywords:

- **Write a sentence or two that summarizes your research topic**

  The City Planning Office in Portland wants to find Web pages on alternative energy. The sentence shown in Figure A-3 demonstrates how to state your research topic.

- **Study the research topic and pull out potential keywords**

  You look at this topic and decide the words that could be used as keywords are *alternative* and *energy*. You circle these words, as shown in Figure A-4. By identifying these words, you are starting to turn your topic statement into terms that an Internet search tool can use effectively. Remember, these are the words you expect to appear on the Web pages that might be useful for your project. Search engines normally do not search for the words *a*, *an*, and *the*. See Table A-2 for typical words that do not qualify as keywords, also known as **stop words**.

- **If necessary, define the keywords and find general background information on your topic**

  Often you may know very little about the topic you are researching. You look in a dictionary and see that alternative energy is considered energy from nonfossil fuels. It mentions *solar* and *wind* as examples. You then look in an encyclopedia to read a bit more about alternative energy. You find other types of alternative energies that might be useful, including *water*, *biomass*, and *geothermal*. Figure A-5 illustrates how to list the keywords you identified for your research topic.

- **Identify synonyms and related terms for the keywords**

  Synonyms are words that have similar meanings. The meanings don't have to be exactly the same, just close. Useful Web pages may have been created by many different people, using different words to describe the same topic. By expanding your list of keywords, you help ensure that your queries are broad enough to find Web pages not indexed under the exact keywords in your initial list. Figure A-6 demonstrates how to list your identified synonyms and related terms.

> **QUICK TIP**
>
> As you review search results, keep this list of keywords and synonyms handy. You might find new words that might be useful if you refine your search later. Also, the words can help you identify topics in the pages you find.

TABLE A-2: Common words that are not normally searched

parts of speech	examples
Articles	a, an, the
Conjunctions and prepositions	and, or, but, in, of, for, on, into, from, than, at, to
Adjectives and adverbs	quick, fine, happy, as, also, probably, however, very
Pronouns and verbs	this, that, these, those, is, be, see, do

FIGURE A-3: Write down your research topic statement

I want to find Web sites about alternative energy.

FIGURE A-4: Circle the keywords in your statement

I want to find Web sites about (alternative)(energy).

FIGURE A-5: Identify and list additional keywords

Keywords

alternative

energy

solar

wind

water

biomass

geothermal

FIGURE A-6: Identify synonyms and related words

Keywords	Synonyms & Related Terms
alternative	renewable, sustainable
energy	power
solar	panels, photovoltaic
wind	turbines, windmills
water	hydropower, hydroelectric
biomass	waste-to-energy, bioenergy
geothermal	heat, pumps

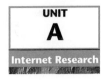

Performing a Basic Search

All search engines offer basic searching; however, they often differ in how they perform the search. It is always a good idea to view each search engine's Help page before you use it. An effective search statement at one search engine may not produce the best results at another. You can overcome these inconsistencies by using a trial-and-error approach to searching. At each search engine, try subtle variations on the search, changing your wording slightly. Note which search engines perform best for different kinds of searches. Over time, you will learn which search engines give you the best results for different subjects. ⬛⬛⬛ Jane thinks you are ready to conduct a basic search. You decide to start with a search for Web pages on solar energy.

STEPS

1. **Open the Data File** IR-UA.doc **in your word-processing program, then save it as** Searching the Internet.doc

   You can use this Data File to keep track of your search results. It is organized by lesson. You will use the same Data File throughout the lessons in this unit, switching between the Data File and your browser as necessary.

2. **Open your browser, go to the Student Online Companion at** www.course.com/illustratedresearch2, **then click the** AOL Search link **(under "Search engines")**

   The AOL Search form appears, as shown in Figure A-7. You are now ready to enter your keywords.

3. **Click the** Search text box, **type** solar energy, **then click the** Search button

   After a moment, your search results appear. Your screen should look similar to Figure A-8.

4. **In the Lesson 4 table in the Data File, record how many pages this search found**

   The number of pages of results appears next to "Matching Sites." Now you decide to alter the search by using the synonym *power* instead of *energy*.

5. **Delete your previous query in the** Search text box, **type** solar power, **press** Enter, **then record how many pages this search found in the Lesson 4 table in the Data File**

   Notice that your browser displays a different number of results for this search than the last. One small change in a search query can radically change the number and quality of search results. You know that using a different search engine can also change your results, so you decide to try your search using Google.

6. **Go to the Student Online Companion at** www.course.com/illustrated/research2, **then click the** Google link **(under "Search engines")**

   The search form for Google appears.

7. **Click the** Google Search text box, **type** solar energy, **then click the** Google Search button

   After a moment, your search results appear.

8. **In the Lesson 4 table in the Data File, record how many Web pages were found, delete your previous query in the** Google Search text box, **type** solar power, **then click the** Google Search button

   Notice that again the browser displays a different number of results for this search than the last. Also, note that the number of results displayed often includes multiple pages per site; that is, a site with multiple pages on your topic may be returned more than once in your results.

9. **In the Lesson 4 table in the Data File, record how many Web pages were found, then save the file**

TROUBLE

Web sites are constantly changing, so if you can't find the exact link or text box cited in the step, look for one that has a similar name or purpose, and if you are still unable to locate the necessary text box or link, see your instructor for assistance.

QUICK TIP

Most search tools allow either pressing Enter or clicking Search to start a search.

QUICK TIP

Be aware that many search engines accept payment for higher placement, so these sites, usually .com sites, are listed where you typically expect the best matching results. Better search engines indicate this, sometimes with the word "Sponsored." However, they are not required to disclose this. The Web site for SearchEngineWatch has information about which engines accept sponsored placement.

FIGURE A-7: AOL Search form

Search text box

Help link

Search button

FIGURE A-8: AOL Search results for *solar energy*

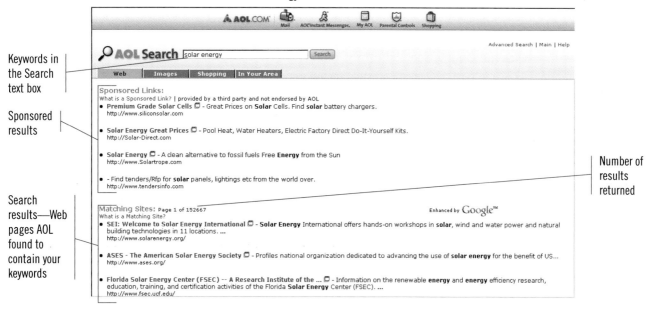

Keywords in the Search text box

Sponsored results

Number of results returned

Search results—Web pages AOL found to contain your keywords

Clues to Use

Why do search results vary with different search engines?

When a search engine spider scans the Internet for Web pages, it finds only a fraction of the Web pages that exist for any given topic. Each engine's spiders crawl different parts of the Web. So when you use a different search engine you are actually searching a slightly different part of the Web. Also, each search engine has unique ranking algorithms. So when your results are ranked for relevancy, different pages may be at the top of the different lists of results.

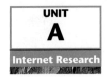
Using Phrases

When you construct a search, you are often looking for two or more words to be in a sentence one right after the other. To find these words in the right order you want to use **phrase searching**. In many search engines, phrase searching is accomplished by putting quotation marks (" ") around the words you want to appear together in your results. Jane suggests that your search can be refined even more with phrase searching. You decide to try a few more searches and compare the results.

STEPS

1. **Go to the Student Online Companion at** www.course.com/illustrated/research2, **then click the** Google link **(under "Search engines")**
   The search form for the Google search engine appears. You are now ready to enter your search.

2. **Click the** Google Search text box, **type** bioenergy center, **then click the** Google Search button
   After a moment, your search results appear.

3. **Use the Lesson 6 table in the Data File to record the number of results this search found**
   You want to try a similar search, with a different word order, to see how the results differ.

4. **Delete the previous query in the** Google Search text box, **type** center bioenergy, **then click the** Google Search button
   After a moment, your search results appear. You should have the same number of results as in your previous search. If *center bioenergy* and *bioenergy center* find the same number of results, then you know you have not limited your search to just the phrase *bioenergy center*. You now use phrase searching to limit the results.

5. **Delete your previous query in the** Google Search text box, **type** "bioenergy center", **then click the** Google Search button
   Be sure to type the quotation marks around the words *"bioenergy center"* to tell Google that you mean to search for an exact phrase. You should now have far fewer results than in the first two searches. You have now located only the Web pages that contain the exact phrase *bioenergy center*. Figure A-9 compares both of the two word searches with the phrase search. Figure A-10 illustrates the results for the phrase search.

6. **Use the Lesson 6 table in the Data File to record your results, then save the Data File**

FIGURE A-9: Searching for the keywords *center bioenergy* both as two words and as a phrase

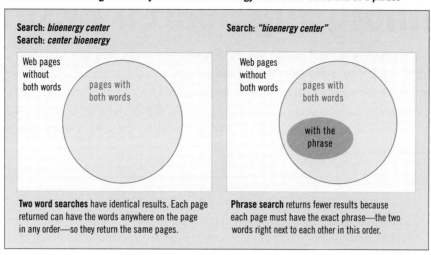

Search: *bioenergy center*
Search: *center bioenergy*

Web pages without both words

pages with both words

Search: *"bioenergy center"*

Web pages without both words

pages with both words

with the phrase

Two word searches have identical results. Each page returned can have the words anywhere on the page in any order—so they return the same pages.

Phrase search returns fewer results because each page must have the exact phrase—the two words right next to each other in this order.

FIGURE A-10: Results for the phrase search *"bioenergy center"*

Quotation marks used around keywords to search as a phrase

Number of search results

Highlighted keyword phrase in results

Internet Research

Clues to Use

Other ways to search using phrases

Most search engines allow phrase searching, but not all in the same way. Many do use quotation marks around words to indicate a phrase. However, some automatically assume you are looking for a phrase when you enter two words in the Search text box. In these search engines, quotation marks are redundant, but harmless. Some search engines provide a drop-down menu or check box with an option for "exact phrase." Others include an additional Search text box labeled "with this exact phrase." Sometimes the option for a phrase search might appear on an advanced search page. Use the Help or Search Tip pages at each search engine to learn how to use phrase searching at that site.

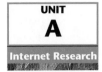

Analyzing Search Results

As you search, you need to scan the results pages to identify Web sites that seem most likely to be useful. Search results pages offer clues that can help you zero in on the best results. Knowing how to navigate and read the results page can save you time as you select from your search results. Figure A-11 points out how to note many of the examples below in your results. ▓▓▓▓▓ Jane has conducted a search using Google on the keyword *geothermal*. She sits down with you to review the search results. She uses the following guidelines in determining the quality of the results.

DETAILS

QUICK TIP

As you search, you will become familiar with domain names. For academic information, use .edu sites. For sites that sell or advocate, look for .com and .org. For professional or association sites, look for .org. For government sites, look for .gov.

- **Locate your search terms within the search result**

  Search engines often display snippets of text from the pages containing your keywords. The number of times your keywords show up in the snippet may indicate the relevance of the Web page to your search. The proximity of the words may also indicate relevance, as would a keyword in the URL. Google displays your search terms in bold for easy scanning.

- **Decipher the URL**

  The name of a URL is often **mnemonic;** that is, it indicates what the Web site is about so that its URL is easier to remember. If the URL contains one of your keywords, it is likely to be mainly about your topic. The end of the domain name (.com, .edu, .jp, .uk, and so on) indicates either a certain type of Web site or its geographic domain. Your first result, which ends in .gov, is a page sponsored by a government agency. If a URL ends in .uk, it is from the United Kingdom. Being aware of this as you scan your results can be very helpful. A search for *domain names* or *country domains* results in lists you can check URLs against.

QUICK TIP

If you want to find the one site Google thinks is the "best," click the I'm Feeling Lucky button.

- **Note the result's ranking in the list of possible Web pages**

  Search engines use **algorithms**, or mathematical formulas, to rank each Web site according to the terms used in your search query. Every search engine has a slightly different algorithm for figuring out which is the "best" Web site, but all place their best picks at the top of the list. Generally speaking, you shouldn't have to go through more than three or four pages of search results to find the pages you want. If you do, try refining your search.

- **Determine if the search engine uses directory links**

  More and more search engines are creating directories (or subject guides) of recommended Web sites on many subjects. If a search engine site has included a Web page in its directory, it may indicate relevance. Clicking a directory link sends you directly to that category of Web pages.

- **Determine if the search engine uses cached pages**

  Sometimes links to Web pages break. Search engines may not become aware of the problem until their spiders search that part of the Web again. As a result, sometimes when you click a link you may get a computer error message. Google has many hidden, or **cached**, copies of indexed Web pages. If you click the word "Cached," you see the copy of the Web page with your keyword(s) highlighted, as shown in Figure A-12. Cached pages can help you find the newer or renamed or relocated version of the page, or find authors' names or other specific terms. Try a new search query using those terms.

- **Navigate between search results pages**

  Search results are usually displayed about 10 to a page. Some searches may return hundreds of pages. At Google you navigate to a different page of results using the links located at the bottom of each results page, as shown in Figure A-13. Google and some other engines also offer search-refining options at the bottom of the page.

FIGURE A-11: Evaluating a search results page

Search for *geothermal*

Result ranked highest for relevancy: *geothermal* in the title, the URL, and on the page

Mnemonic URL

Cached page available

Keyword in URL

Number of results

Google's subject directory categories

Sponsored results

.org and .gov results indicate the kind of material on the pages

Keyword highlighted in results

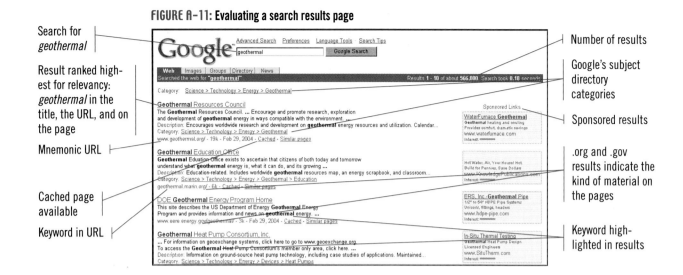

FIGURE A-12: Google's cache of a page from the National Renewable Energy Library

Google notification that this is a cached page

Notice URL's mnemonic name

Keyword highlighted on Web page

URL of and link to the actual Web page

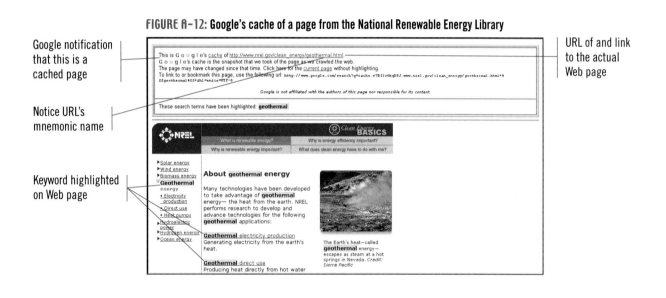

FIGURE A-13: Bottom of Google search results page

Other pages of search results; "best" results should be on the first few pages

Search form provides option to alter search

Use Next link to move to next page of results

Use Search within results link to enter another word or phrase to be searched only within the existing search results

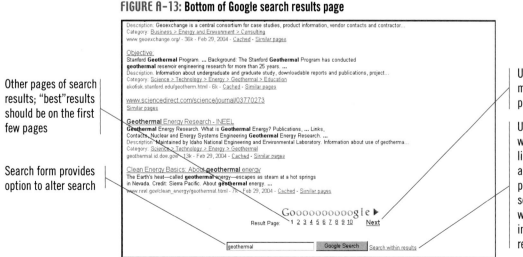

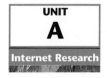

Citing Online Resources

When you use information from Web pages for class work, you need to list them in your works cited. You need to gather enough information about each Web page so that you, or someone reading your paper, can find it later. To present the relevant data about each site consistently, use a recognized citation format. **Citation formats** are style guides that standardize how citations are written. Two widely accepted citation formats are those of the Modern Language Association (MLA) and the American Psychological Association (APA). These style guides provide formats for all kinds of Internet information. See Table A-3 for citation tips. For school work, always check with your instructor to see which style guide format is preferred. ▰▰▰ Jane advises you to use the MLA format to record your citations for the Web pages you are finding about alternative energy.

STEPS

1. **Review the MLA citation format in Figure A-16**

   Figure A-14 shows the elements needed to properly cite a Web page. Figure A-15 shows this format used to cite the Web page in Figure A-16. Different kinds of materials on the Web may have different citation formats. Go to the Student Online Companion at www.course.com/illustrated/research2 to see a list of citation guide links.

2. **Looking at Figure A-16, locate the author and type the name in the Lesson 6 table in the Data File**

   MLA format for author names is surname (last name) first, followed by a comma, then the personal name (first name) followed by a period.

   > **QUICK TIP**
   >
   > Note that many Web pages do not display this information as clearly as this example. You may have to look to find it.

3. **Locate the title of the Web page in Figure A-16 and type it next to the author's name**

   MLA format requires quotation marks around the title with a period at the end of the title.

4. **Find the title of the Web site and type it next to the Web page title**

   MLA format requires the title be underlined and followed by a period.

5. **Look for the date the Web page was created or the date it was last updated**

   Looking at the Web page in Figure A-16, you find no creation date or date last updated. Sometimes this information is not available and you must skip this step.

6. **Type http://science.howstuffworks.com/solar-cell.htm next to the title of the Web site**

   The URL for the Web page is visible in the Address bar of your browser. The URL should be enclosed in angle brackets < > and should not be underlined.

7. **Type the date that you are viewing this Web page**

   The MLA format for dates is *DD Month Abbreviation YYYY* followed by a period. For example: 15 Oct. 2005. It is important to record the date you view a Web page because pages are updated and changed so frequently that information you note might no longer be there a week later.

8. **Compare your citation to the completed example in Figure A-15, make corrections as needed, add your name to the Data File, save, print, and close the Data File, then exit your word-processing program**

   Make sure you have used quotation marks, have underlined the right words, and included all of the required punctuation.

Clues to Use

Copyright and plagiarism

Everything you find on the Internet is copyrighted, whether it is a Web page, an image, or an audio file. If you want to make money using a part of someone else's work, you must get permission from the author or creator. Copyright law is very complex, so you need to consult a lawyer who specializes in copyright law. If you are a student and wish to use part of someone else's work in a school assignment or paper, you generally can do so under the Fair Use exemption to copyright law. This law allows students and researchers to copy or use small parts of other people's creations or writings for educational purposes. You always must give credit by citing the source of the material you are using. If you don't credit an author or source, you are guilty of plagiarism. See Copyright and Plagiarism in the Student Online Companion at www.course.com/illustrated/research2 for more information.

FIGURE A-14: MLA citation format for a Web page

> Author last name, author first name.
>
> "Web PAGE title."
>
> Web SITE title.
>
> Date created or revised.
>
> <Full Internet address>
>
> (Date you viewed the Web page).

FIGURE A-15: Finished MLA style citation for the Web page in Figure A-16

> Aldous, Scott.
> "How Solar Cells Work."
> howstuffworks.
> <http://science.howstuffworks.com/solar-cell.htm>
> (15 Oct. 2005).

FIGURE A-16: Web page for citation: http://science.howstuffworks.com/solar-cell.htm

Web site title

Web page title

Author

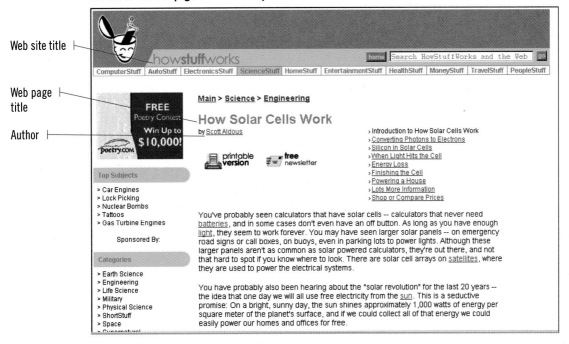

TABLE A-3: Citation tips

citation section	tips
Author	• When authors aren't named, skip this section • If a corporate author is named, such as an association, institution, or government agency, use it in the author section
Page title	• Sometimes the title is not clear; it may be under a banner or logo at the top of the page • If you are citing the whole Web site, you can skip this section, which is for a specific page
URL	• The URL should not be underlined • Some word processors automatically underline URLs, so you may need to remove the underline
Date created/revised	• Sometimes a date can be difficult to find; it may be at the very bottom of the page • When dates aren't provided, skip this section
Date viewed	• If you print the page, the date is at the bottom right-hand corner of your printout • If you are not printing, note the date for your citation

Practice

▼ CONCEPTS REVIEW

Label each element of Figure A-17.

FIGURE A-17

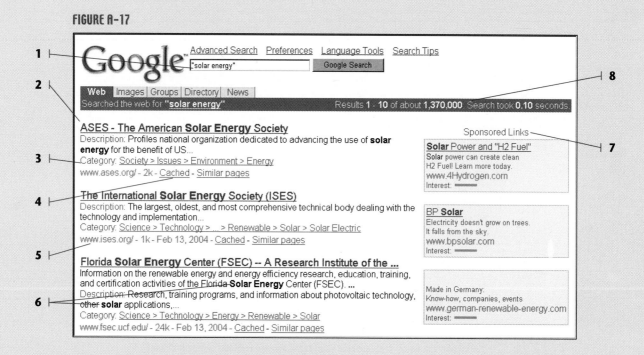

Match each term with the statement that best describes it.

9. Results ranking
10. Cached page
11. Search engine
12. Keywords
13. Sponsored links
14. Search tools
15. Synonyms

a. A Web site that locates information on the Internet by searching Web pages
b. Words that describe your search topic
c. Web pages that have paid for higher placement on search result pages
d. The order in which a search tool returns results, usually based on relevancy
e. Copy of a Web page stored by a search engine
f. Words that have similar meanings
g. Service that helps you find information on the Internet and the Web

Select the best answer from the following list of choices.

16. Which is *not* a step in the research strategy?
   a. Defining your research topic
   b. Choosing the proper Internet search tool
   c. Entering keywords without preparation
   d. Evaluating your search results

17. Phrase searching helps you find:

   a. Words in the order you specify.

   b. Keywords.

   c. Wildcards.

   d. Synonyms.

18. Which is *not* part of an MLA citation for a generic Web page?

   a. Author's first name

   b. Web page title

   c. City from which Web page is published

   d. URL

▼ SKILLS REVIEW

1. Understand Internet search tools.

   a. Open the Data File SR-UA.doc, type **your name** in the space provided, and save it as **IR Skills Review-UA.doc**.

   b. In the Skill #1 box in the table, write a paragraph describing the four common Internet search tools.

   c. Save the Data File.

2. Create an Internet research strategy.

   a. In the Skill #2 box in the table, type the seven steps of the research strategy in order.

   b. Write a paragraph in the Skill #2 table in the Data File addressing the importance of translating your topic into a search query and the value of refining your query to retrieve better results.

   c. Save the Data File.

3. Identify the right keywords.

   a. You have defined your search topic as follows: I want to find information about the <u>history</u> of <u>cotton</u> <u>farming</u>.

   b. Type the topic in the Skill #3 box in the Data File.

   c. Boldface or underline the three keywords in the topic.

   d. List the three keywords below the topic.

   e. Think of at least three synonyms or related words for the keywords (three total—they might all be synonyms for the same keyword).

   f. Use the Data File to enter the synonyms and related words next to the appropriate keywords.

   g. Save the Data File.

4. Perform a basic search.

   a. You have decided to search for **cotton plantations**.

   b. Open your Internet browser, go to the Student Online Companion at www.course.com/illustrated/research2, then click the Google link.

   c. Perform the search **cotton plantations**.

   d. Note the number of search results in the Skill #4 box in the Data File.

   e. Save the Data File.

5. Use phrases.

   a. Go to the Student Online Companion at www.course.com/illustrated/research2, then click the Google link.

   b. Search for the phrase *"cotton plantations"* with quotation marks around your keywords.

   c. Use the Skill #5 box in the Data File to record the number of search results.

   d. Save the Data File.

6. Analyze search results.

   a. Go to the Student Online Companion at www.course.com/illustrated/research2 and click the Google link.

   b. Search for *cotton*.

   c. Look over your search results.

   d. Record the total number of results in the Skill #6 table in the Data File.

   e. Record the number of pages listed on the first page of results that contain your keyword in the URL in the Skill #7 table in the Data File.

   f. Record the number of pages that have paid to be listed on the first page of results.

   g. Record the number of pages listed on the first page of results that Google has cached.

   h. Record whether or not Google displays your search term in bold in each result.

   i. Save the Data File.

7. Cite online resources.

   a. Select one of the Web pages returned by one of the above cotton-related searches.

   b. Print the page you plan to cite.

   c. Use the Skill #7 table in the Data File to create an MLA format Web page citation.

   d. Add *your name* to the Data File, save it, then print it. Close the file and exit your word-processing program.

▼ INDEPENDENT CHALLENGE 1

You want to find information on the Internet about skiing in British Columbia. You want to try a few different searches to see which finds the best information.

   a. Go to the Student Online Companion at www.course.com/illustrated/research2, and click the link for the Google search engine.

   b. Perform the keyword search *skiing British Columbia*.

   c. Record the number of search results in a text file with your name at the top, and save it as *Unit A IC1.doc*.

   d. Perform the keyword search *British Columbia skiing*.

   e. Record the number of results in the text file

   f. Perform the phrase search *"British Columbia skiing"*.

   g. Record the number of results in the text file.

   h. In the text file, write a few sentences explaining which search you thought was the best and why the phrase search found fewer results.

Advanced Challenge Exercise

You decide to find sites that mention all types of snow sports in British Columbia.

   ■ Perform the search: *"British Columbia" skiing*

   ■ Perform the search: *"British Columbia" "cross country skiing"*

   ■ Perform the search: *"British Columbia" snowboarding*

   ■ Perform the search: *"British Columbia" snowshoeing*

   ■ Perform the search: *"British Columbia" skiing "cross country skiing" snowboarding snowshoeing*

   ■ In the text file, record the number of results for each of these five searches.

   i. Add *your name* to the file, save it, print it, close the file and exit your word-processing program.

▼ INDEPENDENT CHALLENGE 2

Your friend is considering a career change and wants you to help with a Web search. The topic statement is: I want to find information about careers in computing in Great Britain.

    a. Type the topic in a word processor and save it as **Unit A IC2.doc**.

    b. Boldface or underline the keywords in the topic.

    c. Copy each keyword onto a separate line.

    d. Adjacent to each keyword, type all synonyms and related words you know.

    e. From all of your keywords, compose a search and type it on the next line (make sure to include the stemmed word with the wildcard in the search).

    f. Go to the Student Online Companion at www.course.com/illustrated/research2, then click the link for Yahoo.

    g. Perform your search, then record the number of search results in your file.

    h. Add **your name** to the file, save it, print it, close the file and exit your word-processing program.

▼ INDEPENDENT CHALLENGE 3

You want to find information on the Internet.

    a. Decide on a topic and describe it in a sentence or two.

    b. Decide on the keywords, synonyms, and related terms.

    c. Develop a search query, choose a search engine, and perform a search.

    d. Analyze the search results, and if necessary, refine your search query and perform the refined search.

    e. When satisfied with the results, print the first page of results, and write your name at the top.

    f. In a text file that you save as **Unit A IC3.doc**, describe how you analyzed your results.

    g. Select one of the returned Web pages, and in the same text file, create a citation for it in the MLA format.

    h. Save the text file, type your name at the top, then print the text file and attach it to your results printout. Close the file and exit your word-processing program.

▼ INDEPENDENT CHALLENGE 4

You decide to choose a topic and compare search results of the same search using two different search engines.

    a. Decide on a topic and enter it in a sentence or two in a text file that you save as **Unit A IC4.doc**.

    b. Identify the keywords, synonyms, and related terms, then record them in the text file.

    c. Choose one keyword and search for it using two different search engines of your choice.

    d. Use the text file to record the number of results from each search.

    e. Using the Help pages, read about searching at both engines.

    f. In the same text file, describe not only how the search engines are different or similar, but also how their results pages are different or similar.

Advanced Challenge Exercise

    ■ Choose a keyword phrase from your previous search, and using quotation marks, perform searches with it at the same two search engines.

    ■ Look over the first page of results from each search and compare them.

    ■ In the same text file, write a new paragraph outlining the comparisons and what conclusions you can make from them.

    ■ Chose one Web page returned for your search and cite it in MLA format in the text file.

    g. Add **your name** to the file, then save and print the file. Close the file and exit your word-processing program.

Internet Research

▼ VISUAL WORKSHOP

You are an ice hockey fan, and a friend gives you a printout of this great Web page, but the URL that should be at the bottom of the page is torn off. You decide to find the page from the information you do have on the printout. You decide to search for the page and record the relevant information in the MLA citation format so you can find it again easily in the future. In a search engine(s) of your choice, search for the Web page shown in Figure A-18. In your word-processing software, create the citation for this Web page. Add **your name** to the file, save it as **Unit A VW.doc**, print the file and exit your word-processing program.

FIGURE A-18

Constructing Complex Searches

OBJECTIVES

Understand Boolean operators
Narrow the search with the AND operator
Expand the search with the OR operator
Restrict queries with the AND NOT operator
Use multiple Boolean operators
Search with filters
Combine Boolean operators and filters
Use metasearch engines

In the previous unit, you learned how to perform a basic search using keywords and phrases. However, many search engines allow more complex queries, sometimes called advanced searches. A **complex query** uses special connecting words and symbols called Boolean operators to define the relationships between your keywords and phrases. **Boolean operators**, such as AND, OR, and AND NOT, let you expand, narrow, or restrict your searches based on Boolean logic. **Boolean logic**, or Boolean algebra, is the field of mathematics that defines how Boolean operators manipulate large sets of data. Because search engines handle large data sets, most of them support Boolean logic and complex query statements. **Search filters** provide another method to narrow your search by limiting its scope to a specific part of the Web. Combining complex query statements with search filters lets you conduct complex or advanced searches that focus more exactly on your target. You can also use a metasearch engine to search multiple search engines' indexes simultaneously to get very broad search results. ▨▨▨ The Portland City Planning team reviews the results from the searches you have conducted on solar energy as an alternative energy resource. The team thinks this is a viable resource, and wants more information on solar energy associations in the Portland, Oregon, area. They also want to know if any surrounding states use solar energy as a resource. Finally, one of the team members expresses an interest in learning about wind as an alternative energy source. To meet the team's request, Jane suggests using Boolean operators and filters to refine your searching.

Understanding Boolean Operators

The English language has a set of rules, or **syntax**, for combining words to form grammatical sentences. Many search engines rely on a special mathematical syntax, called Boolean logic, for constructing complex queries. In Boolean logic, keywords act like nouns in an English sentence. Like nouns, keywords represent your subject. Boolean operators are like conjunctions in an English sentence: they define the connections between keywords. Boolean logic is usually illustrated with Venn diagrams. Jane suggests you review the following information on Venn diagrams to help you understand how to use Boolean operators. Jane assures you Boolean operators can help you develop more precise searches.

DETAILS

QUICK TIP
Whenever you have trouble deciding which Boolean operator to use in your search strategy, take the time to sketch a Venn diagram labeled with your terms and it will become clear.

QUICK TIP
Always use all CAPITAL LETTERS when typing any Boolean operator. If you type the word *and* in lowercase, it might be interpreted as a keyword rather than as the Boolean operator AND.

QUICK TIP
If you're unsure about using Boolean operators at a new search engine or unsure about its default operator, refer to the Help pages.

To review Boolean operators and Venn diagrams:

- Venn diagrams

  Venn diagrams are drawings that are used to create a visual representation of a search using Boolean operators. For example, consider the illustration in Figure B-1 in which the rectangle represents the World Wide Web. Circles inside the rectangle represent groups of related Web pages, called **sets**. These circles, or sets, can also represent your searches. One circle represents a search for pages containing the word *cats*. Another circle represents a search for *dogs*. If the circles overlap, the overlapping area represents pages that are retrieved by both searches. This overlapping area is called the **intersection** of the sets. If you limit your search to pages containing *both* the words, the search results are represented by the intersection of these two circles. If you expand your search to pages containing *either* word, the search results are represented by both full circles. This is called the **union** of the two sets. If you restrict your search to pages containing one word, but *not* the other one, this search is represented by the part of one circle that does *not* overlap the other one. This search excludes one set from the other.

- Common Boolean operators: AND, OR, and AND NOT

  The most common Boolean operators are the words AND, OR, and AND NOT. They act as commands to the search engine by connecting keywords and phrases it uses to retrieve the results you want. They tell the engine which keywords *must* be on the Web page (AND); which *may or may not* be on the Web page (OR); and which keyword *must not* be on the Web page (AND NOT).

- Default Boolean operator

  Search engines insert Boolean operators into multiple word searches whether supplied in the search query or not. The operator that the engine automatically uses is called the **default operator**. Many search engines default to AND. Others default to OR. When you search two or more words, some engines assume you want the words in a phrase, and so they treat the query as if you used quotation marks. Being aware of an engine's default operator is important to create the best search strategy for that engine.

- Where to use Boolean operators

  Some search engines allow Boolean searching on the basic search page, but some allow it only on the advanced search page. In the past, almost all search engines recognized all Boolean operators when typed in all capital letters in the Search text box on the basic search page. Now many only recognize them if you use the advanced search page's specialized text boxes. Or, they may not use the English words AND or NOT, but may allow the plus sign (+) or minus sign (–) instead.

Clues to Use

Keep a search diary

Boolean search statements provide a standardized way of noting your searches. It is a good idea to log searches as you perform them, noting the Boolean operators. This helps you remember what searches you have tried and which ones yielded useful results. Your search logs can even be used by others to reproduce your search results.

FIGURE B-1: Venn diagrams of Boolean logic

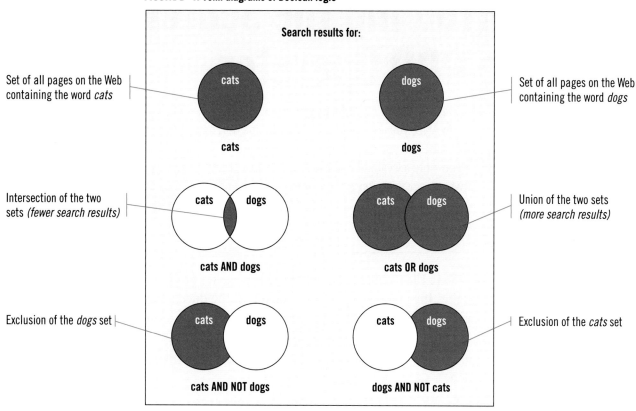

Search results for:

Set of all pages on the Web containing the word *cats*

cats

Set of all pages on the Web containing the word *dogs*

dogs

Intersection of the two sets *(fewer search results)*

cats AND dogs

Union of the two sets *(more search results)*

cats OR dogs

Exclusion of the *dogs* set

cats AND NOT dogs

Exclusion of the *cats* set

dogs AND NOT cats

Clues to Use

Where have you heard this before?

You might remember Boolean logic and Venn diagrams from a math class. George Boole (1815–1864), an Englishman, invented a form of symbolic logic called Boolean Algebra, which is used in the fields of mathematics, logic, computer science, and artificial intelligence. John Venn (1843–1923), also an Englishman, used his diagrams to explain visually what Boole had described symbolically—the intersection, union, and exclusion of sets. Little did they know then that they were creating the foundation of the language that Internet search engines use today.

Narrowing the Search with the AND Operator

The Boolean operator AND is a powerful operator that limits your results. Whenever you connect keywords in your search with AND, you are telling the search engine that *both* of the keywords must be on every Web page. Each AND added to your search query further narrows the search results to fewer pages. However, these pages will be more relevant than those returned by a broader, or less specific, search. So, the best time to use AND is when your initial keyword or phrase search finds too many irrelevant results. Table B-1 provides more information on the AND operator. 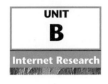 Jane suggests you start searching with Boolean operators. You decide to start with AND in a search for solar energy associations near you in Portland.

STEPS

1. **Open the Data File** IR-UB.doc **in your word-processing program, save it as** Complex Searches.doc, **then type** your name **at the top of the document**
   This document contains a table that you can use to record your search results.

2. **Open your browser, go to the Student Online Companion at** www.course.com/illustrated/research2, **then click the** Google link
   The Google Basic Search page appears.

3. **Click the** Google Search text box, **type** "solar energy association" **then click the** Google Search button
   Your search results appear.

4. **Use the Lesson 2 table in the Data File to record the number of search results**
   Noting the number of results will illustrate how Boolean operators can broaden or narrow a search.

5. **Delete the first search in the Google Search text box, type** Portland **in the** Google Search text box, **then click the** Google Search button
   In a moment, your search results appear.

6. **Use the Lesson 2 table in the Data File to record the number of search results**
   To find the pages that contain *both* the name *Portland* and the phrase *"solar energy association"* you would have to read as many Web pages as these two resulting sets combined. But you realize you can create a search strategy using a Boolean operator to identify these pages for you.

7. **Delete the search in the Google Search text box, type** "solar energy association" AND Portland, **then click the** Google Search button
   This search, using the AND operator, narrows your results to *solar energy association* pages that also contain *Portland*. Figure B-2 is a diagram of this search. Figure B-3 illustrates the search results. This search is meant to make you conscious of using the Boolean operator AND. Note, however, that Google uses AND as its default operator, so in this case entering it in your search was unnecessary. But as a practice, you should either enter the AND operator or use the Advanced Search pages that provide specialized text boxes.

8. **Use the Lesson 2 table in the Data File to record the number of search results, then save the document**

FIGURE B-2: Venn diagram illustrating results for: "solar energy association" AND Portland

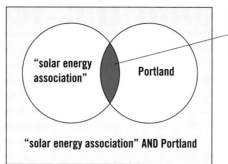

Web pages containing both "solar energy association" and Portland (the intersection of the two sets)

"solar energy association" AND Portland

FIGURE B-3: Google search: "solar energy association" AND Portland

Your query

Number of results

How your query was interpreted and searched

TABLE B-1: The Boolean operator AND

when to use	• When finding too many irrelevant results • To focus or narrow or limit a search • To force the search of a stop word
variations	• AND • Plus sign (+)
searches	• Most basic searches allow AND and/or the plus sign (+) • Advanced searches usually use a list box, check box, or specialized text box, often with words like: "must include" or "all of the words"
sample uses	• **use:** *solar* AND *panels*; **result:** narrows search; decreases number of results • **use:** "*+The +Apartment*"; **result:** forces inclusion of the stop word 'The' in a phrase

Clues to Use

The plus sign

Many search engines use the plus sign (+) to represent the AND operator. So, instead of entering the English word AND as the Boolean operator, you can enter the symbol (+). This tells the engine that this word must be on every page. There must be a space in front of the plus sign but no space between it and the term it is connecting to the first term. For example: *solar +energy +Portland* is the same search as *solar* AND *energy* AND *Portland*. The plus sign is also useful to prevent a search engine ignoring a stop word. For example, *Henry + I* should produce the same results as "*Henry I.*" Here it functions like quotation marks around a phrase. In both cases, it forces the search engine to look for a word it would normally ignore.

Expanding the Search with the OR Operator

As you have seen, the AND Boolean operator *narrows* your search. Conversely, the Boolean operator OR expands your results. When you connect keywords in your search with OR, you are telling the search engine to find any of the keywords on every Web page. In other words, every page returned must have at least one of the keywords on it. Each OR added to your search expands the search to include more Web pages. A good time to use OR is when your initial search finds too few results. Refer back to the synonyms or related words you identified when developing your search strategy and connect one or more to your search with OR. Table B-2 has more information about the OR operator. ▓▓▓▓▓ A team member at the City Planning Office asked you to find information on wind energy. You decide to locate Web pages that contain either *"wind turbines"* or *"wind energy."* Jane suggests you use the OR Boolean operator for this search.

STEPS

TROUBLE
If your browser is not at Google, go to the Student Online Companion at www.course.com/illustrated/research2, then click the Google link.

1. **At the Google site type** "wind turbines" **in the Google Search text box, then click the** Google Search button

   Before performing your Boolean OR search, you want to search the keywords alone to compare results.

2. **Use the Lesson 3 table in the Data File to record the number of search results**

3. **Delete your previous query in the Google Search text box, type** "wind energy", **then click the** Google Search button

4. **Use the Lesson 3 table in the Data File to record the number of search results**

   Now you want to compare these results to a search connecting the two search phrases with the OR operator.

QUICK TIP
If you were to add a third keyword with the OR operator, your results would be even larger, because OR broadens your search. So, more results are returned for: "wind energy" OR "wind turbines" OR "wind mills".

5. **Delete your previous query in the Google Search text box, type** "wind energy" OR "wind turbines", **then click the** Google Search button

   After a moment, your search results appear. Figure B-4 illustrates your search results with a Venn diagram. This search combines the results of both of your previous searches. Figure B-5 shows Google's search results page. You might reasonably expect the number of results to be significantly higher than it is, since the OR expands the search. It is somewhat lower than expected because some Web pages contain both phrases and the results page eliminates many duplicates. This search is meant to make you conscious of using the Boolean operator OR. Be aware that some search engines use OR as a default operator, in which case entering it in your search would be unnecessary. But as a practice, you should either enter the OR operator or use Advanced Search pages that provide specialized text boxes.

6. **Use the Lesson 3 table in the Data File to record the number of search results, then save the document**

FIGURE B-4: Venn diagram illustrating results for: "wind turbines" OR "wind energy"

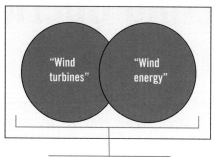

Web pages containing either
keyword phrase

FIGURE B-5: Google search: "wind turbines" OR "wind energy"

Keyword
phrases
highlighted in
search results

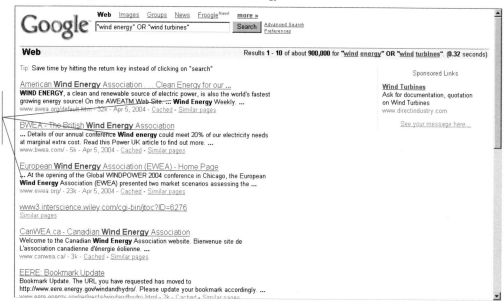

TABLE B-2: The Boolean operator OR

when to use	• When finding too few results • To broaden a search • To combine synonyms or related terms
searches	• Most basic searches allow OR • Advanced searches usually use a list box, check box, or specialized text box, often with words like: "any of the words" or "with at least one of the words"
sample uses	• **use:** *Oregon* OR *Northwest*; **result:** broadens search; increases number of results • **use:** *renewable* OR *sustainable*; **result:** combines related words

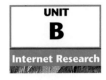

Restricting Queries with the AND NOT Operator

The Boolean operator AND NOT excludes the keyword or phrase that follows it. Therefore, AND NOT narrows or limits your search. When you add AND NOT and an additional keyword to a search strategy, fewer results are returned. Use the AND NOT operator if your initial search returns too many irrelevant or unhelpful results. When you scan the first couple of results pages and see numerous irrelevant pages returned, try to locate any words or phrases that your desired search results should *not* contain. This is a good time to identify a category of results you do *not* want to retrieve and add it to your search with AND NOT. Table B-3 provides more information about using AND NOT. ▰▰▰▰▰ You have been reviewing your search results for solar energy associations in Portland. You notice they include Web pages about two cities—Portland, Oregon, and Portland, Maine. You are only interested in associations in Portland, Oregon. Jane suggests you conduct another search to eliminate the pages that refer to Portland, Maine.

STEPS

1. **At the Google site, click the** Google Search text box, **type** "solar energy association" AND Portland, **then click the** Google Search button

    Before performing your Boolean AND NOT search, you decide to search without it to compare results. After a few moments, your search results appear. Again, the results include Web pages about both cities—Portland, Oregon, and Portland, Maine.

2. **Use the Lesson 4 table in the Data File to record the number of search results**

    Now you want to use AND NOT to exclude Web pages about Portland, Maine. In Google, you must use the minus sign (–) for the Boolean operator AND NOT.

3. **Click immediately after the word** Portland **in the Google Search text box, type** -Maine, **then click the** Google Search button

    Be sure to not leave a space between the minus sign and the word *Maine*. Figure B-6 is a diagram of your search. After a moment, your search results appear. The page should look similar to the one in Figure B-7. Note that this search returned fewer results. That is because your search excluded every page that contained the word *Maine*.

4. **Use the Lesson 4 table in the Data File to record the number of search results, then save the document**

Clues to Use

More on the AND NOT operator

You may encounter this operator referred to as: AND NOT, as AND-NOT, as NOT, and as the minus sign (-). However it is written, the Boolean logic is the same—it excludes the following word or phrase from the search results. A search tool's Help pages or Advanced Search pages should provide information about how it understands Boolean operators. For example, many search engines recognize the hyphen, or minus sign (-), and interpret it to mean the Boolean AND NOT. Use a space before the hyphen (-) and do not leave a space between it and the word it is connecting to the search query. So, a search for *cats* AND NOT *dogs* retrieves the same results as the search *cats -dogs*.

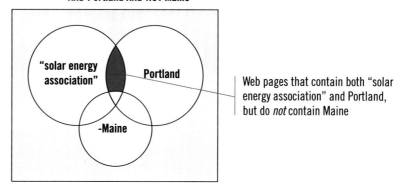

FIGURE B-6: Venn diagram illustrating results for: "solar energy association" AND Portland AND NOT Maine

Web pages that contain both "solar energy association" and Portland, but do *not* contain Maine

FIGURE B-7: Google search results for: "solar energy association" AND Portland AND NOT Maine

AND NOT search to exclude pages containing the word Maine

TABLE B-3: The Boolean operator AND NOT

when to use	• To focus or narrow or limit a search • To exclude a concept • When finding too many irrelevant results
variations	• AND NOT • Hyphen or minus sign (-)
searches	• Most basic searches allow the hyphen or minus sign (-) • Advanced searches usually use a list box, check box, or specialized text box, often with words like: "must not include" or "without the words"
sample use	• **use:** "*alternative energy*" AND NOT *geothermal*; **result:** excludes one concept; decreases number of results

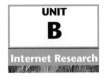

Using Multiple Boolean Operators

Combining Boolean operators in your search strategy provides more focused results. You can use operators in any logical combination. When searching with more than one set of keywords, use parentheses to tell the search tool which words belong together. When using more than one operator, use parentheses to force the order in which the search is performed. Unless the query instructs search tools to do otherwise, the query is read and the operators performed from left to right. When you use parentheses, you instruct the search tool to perform the part of the search inside the parentheses first. This is called **forcing the order of operation**. Using parentheses has a significant impact on search results. Figure B-8 illustrates results in which the search tool read the query and performed the search from left to right, producing irrelevant results. Figure B-9 illustrates results in which the order of operation was forced, producing relevant results. The team at the Portland City Planning Office also wants information on solar energy resources from the surrounding region, not just in Portland, Oregon. Jane suggests you combine Boolean operators in a complex search. But first you search the two sets of keywords separately so you can compare your results.

STEPS

1. **At the Google site, click the** Google Search text box, **type** "Washington state" OR "British Columbia" OR "Pacific Northwest", **then click the** Google Search button

   You learned on previous searches that if you just enter *Washington* your results contain many pages referring to Washington D.C., so you alter your strategy to include the word *state*. Your results appear.

2. **Use the Lesson 5 table in the Data File to record the number of search results**

3. **Delete your previous query in the Google Search text box, type** "solar energy", **click the** Google Search button, **then use the Lesson 5 table in the Data File to record the number of search results**

   After a moment, your search results appear. Now you need to combine and limit these results to Web pages about solar energy that also refer to the Northwest, but do not refer to Oregon. You use parentheses to tell Google which sets of words belong together.

4. **Click the** Google Search text box, **edit your search to read:** "solar energy" (Washington OR "British Columbia" OR "Pacific Northwest") -Oregon, **then click the** Google Search button

   Notice that, because Google defaults to the AND operator, you do not need to enter AND between the phrase and the keywords in parentheses. In a search engine that defaults to OR, you need to enter the AND or the plus sign (+). Notice also that you must use the minus sign (–) for Google to understand you mean AND NOT. Your search results appear. Figure B-10 illustrates the results in a Venn diagram.

5. **Use the Lesson 5 table in the Data file to record the number of search results, then save the document**

FIGURE B-8: Venn diagram illustrating the incorrect search: constitution +American OR "United States"

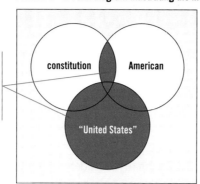

Order of operation was *not* forced with parentheses, so the search engine read the operators from left to right, resulting in Web pages containing "constitution" and American and then or "United States"

FIGURE B-9: Venn diagram illustrating the search: constitution +(American OR "United States")

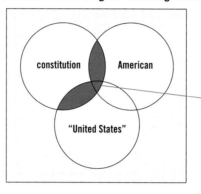

Order of operation *was* forced with parentheses, so the part of the search inside the parentheses was read first, resulting in Web pages containing "constitution" and then either American or "United States"

FIGURE B-10: Venn diagram illustrating results for: "solar energy" +("Washington state" OR "British Columbia" OR "Pacific Northwest") -Oregon

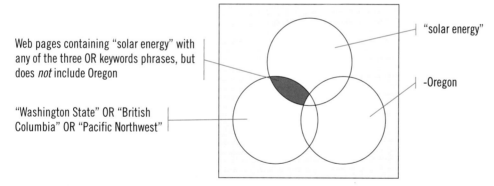

Web pages containing "solar energy" with any of the three OR keywords phrases, but does *not* include Oregon

"Washington State" OR "British Columbia" OR "Pacific Northwest"

"solar energy"

-Oregon

Clues to Use

Planning a complex search

You can combine Boolean operators to develop a complex search strategy. For example: If you want to use Google to search alternative energy in British Columbia or Alberta, Canada, but do *not* want pages on geothermal energy, here are sample steps to develop an effective strategy:

1. Identify the first concept. Use keywords, synonyms, and related words. Connect them with OR and surround them with parentheses.

   (British Columbia OR BC OR Alberta)

2. Identify the second concept. Use keywords/synonyms/related words, and connect them with OR and surround them with parentheses.

   (Canada OR Canadian)

3. Identify the third concept. Quotation marks identify this as a phrase.

   "alternative energy"

4. Identify the fourth concept. You want this word excluded from your results, so you use the Boolean operator AND NOT. Google uses the minus sign (–) as AND NOT.

   –geothermal

5. Connect all of your concepts into one search statement:

   (British Columbia OR BC OR Alberta) AND (Canada OR Canadian) AND "alternative energy" -geothermal

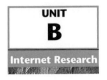

Searching with Filters

Another way to refine a search is to use filters. **Filters** are programs that tell search tools to screen out specified types of Web pages or files. They are usually located on Advanced Search pages. As you develop your search strategy, use filters to search only a specified area of the Web or to exclude specified areas of the Web. For example, you use language filters to search only for pages in English, or date filters to search only for pages updated in the last year, or for certain file types like images, audio, or video. Table B-4 lists examples of filter options available on Google's Advanced Search page. ▨▨▨▨ Your colleague at the Portland City Planning Office tells you that Denmark is a leader in wind power. You would like to see some Danish sites, but because you don't read Danish, you need to find pages that are in English. Jane suggests you use filters to focus the search. To use filters, you go to an Advanced Search page.

STEPS

1. **At the Google site, click** Advanced Search

   The Google Advanced Search page appears displaying the Google filter options. Google also provides special filter options for searching images and groups on the Advanced Image Search page and Advanced Groups Search page.

2. **Click the** Language list box, **then click** English

   English should be selected, as shown in Figure B-11. With this filter selected, your search results will only include Web pages written in English. Now you want to restrict your search to the domain exclusive to Denmark. You searched earlier and found that .dk is the domain for Demark.

QUICK TIP

The Domains filter lets you choose between "*Only* return results from the site or domain" or "*Don't* return results from the site or domain." In this search, you want it to read *Only*.

3. **Type** .dk **in the Domains filter text box**

   The Domains text box should appear as shown in Figure B-11. With this filter selected, your search results will only include Web pages from Denmark.

4. **Type** wind power **in the** with the exact phrase text box **then click the** Google Search button

   Quotation marks are not needed to indicate a phrase search. This specialized text box interprets any words typed into it as a phrase, so quotation marks are assumed. Figure B-12 illustrates the results in a Venn diagram. The Web pages returned contain the phrase *wind power*, are in English, and are from Denmark's domain.

5. **Use the Lesson 6 table in the Data File to record the number of search results, then save the Data File**

   Note that Google has translated your search as *"wind power" site:.dk*. Quotation marks show how Google interpreted the words you typed into the "with the exact phrase" box. The *site:.dk* is how Google translated your domain filter selection. Just below the tabs you see that Google searched only pages in English. Google reiterates your query as Searched *English* pages for *"wind power" site:.dk*. Check this information to determine if the filters worked the way you expected when you developed the search strategy.

TABLE B-4: Examples of filters at Google's Advanced Search page

Language	Limits search to pages written in the language you choose (English, French, Japanese, etc.)
File Format	Limits search to pages in the format you choose (.pdf, .xls, .doc, etc.)
Date	Limits search to pages updated within a specified time period (3, 6, or 12 months)
Occurrences	Limits search to pages containing your keywords in the location you choose (URL, title, links, etc.)
Domain	Limits search to include pages only with a specified domain or to exclude pages with a specified domain
Safe Search	Limits search by filtering to exclude potentially offensive pages (can be hit and miss)

Phrase search for wind power

Language filter selected for English

Domain filter selected for .dk, Denmark's domain

Specialized search text boxes for Boolean logic

Filters

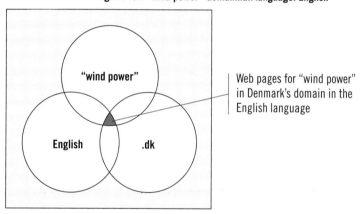

FIGURE B-12: Venn diagram for: "wind power" domain:.dk language: English

Web pages for "wind power" in Denmark's domain in the English language

Clues to Use

Filtering domains in the URL

Filters search only for letters or words that appear in certain parts of a URL. The final two or three letters in the URL indicate domains. Web sites in the United States have URLs that end in three letters that represent the type of organization hosting the Web site. For example: university sites end in .edu; government sites end in .gov; commercial sites end in .com; and nonprofits end in .org. Others include: .biz, .pro, .info, .net, .us, .coop, .museum, and

.name. Web sites located in other countries use 2-letter country codes: Canada's domain is .ca; the United Kingdom's domain is .uk; Japan's domain is .jp. Any of these 2- or 3-letter codes can limit search results when using a domain filter. For a full listing of the 2-letter country codes, go to www.iana.org/cctld/cctld-whois.htm. You can find other sites with this information by searching for: *countries* AND *domains*.

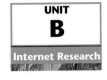
Combining Boolean Operators and Filters

Most search tools provide Advanced Search pages that make entering complex searches easier. These pages allow you to combine Boolean operators and filters to create complex, very specific searches that return relevant results. ▓▓▓▓▓ Before your next meeting with the team at the Portland City Planning Office, you need to identify some Canadian pages on alternative energies, other than geothermal, and that are in the PDF file format, because they are easy to reproduce. You are not sure how to formulate such a specific search query, so you ask Jane for guidance. Jane guides you in developing a search strategy utilizing both Boolean operators and filters. Table B-5 outlines your strategy.

STEPS

1. **At the Google site, click** Advanced Search, **click the** with all of the words text box, **and type** university energy

    As you saw in the last lesson, Google provides special text boxes for Boolean searching and mostly list boxes for searching with filters. This text box represents the AND Boolean operator. You do not need to type the AND.

2. **Click the** with at least one of the words text box, **and type** alternative sustainable renewable

    This text box represents the OR Boolean operator. You do not need to type the OR.

3. **Click the** without the words text box, **and type** geothermal

    This text box represents the AND NOT Boolean operator. You do not need to type the AND NOT.

4. **In the** Language list box, **select** English

    This list box filters for Web pages written only in the language you choose.

5. **In the** File Format list box, **select** Only, **then select** Adobe Acrobat PDF (.pdf)

    This list box filters for Web pages that are only in the file format you choose.

6. **In the** Domain filter list box, **select** Only, **then type** .ca **in the text box**

    This list box filters for Web pages that are only located in the domain you choose.

7. **Compare your screen to Figure B-13 to make sure your selections match those in the figure, then click the** Google Search button

    When the search results appear, notice that near the top of the page Google restates your search. A quick check of this information verifies the Boolean text boxes and the filters worked as you expected.

8. **Use the Lesson 7 table in the Data File to record the number of search results, then save the file**

> **QUICK TIP**
> Even with a fast Internet connection, a complex search using several different operators and filters can take noticeably longer to present results than a simpler search.

Clues to Use

Using the search text boxes on an Advanced Search page

When using Advanced Search text boxes, you do not actually type AND, OR, AND NOT, (+), or (–). When using these specialized text boxes, the search engine understands the operator you want to use so you can enter multiple words without the operators. However, if you need to enter a phrase in the OR box, you need to use quotation marks around the phrase and place a plus sign (+) in front of the words inside the quotation marks. The first word in each phrase does not require the plus sign, but you may want to make a practice of using it in front of any word in a phrase to help you remember a plus sign is needed on every word after the first word. For example, to search for *solar panels* or *wind turbines* on Google's Advanced Search form, enter: "+solar +panels" "+wind +turbines" in the OR box. This ensures your search is interpreted as two phrases rather than four words.

FIGURE B-13: Google Advanced Search page using filters and Boolean operators

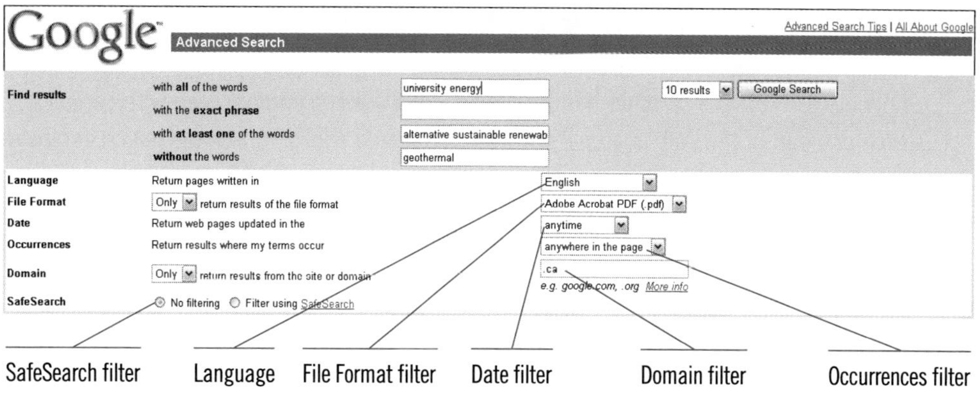

TABLE B-5: Planning a complex search using both Boolean operators and filters

You would like to identify some Canadian domain pages, in PDF format, on alternative energies other than geothermal. To use Google for this search, here are the steps to develop your strategy combining Boolean operators and filters:

1. Identify the first concept. Connect keywords with OR and surround them with parentheses.	(alternative OR renewable OR sustainable)
2. Identify the second concept. Use keywords/synonyms/related words, and connect them with OR and surround them with parentheses.	(energy OR energies)
3. Identify the third concept.	-geothermal
4. Use filters as needed.	Language: English Domain: .ca File Format: .pdf

One way to record your search strategy:

       (alternative OR renewable OR sustainable) (energy OR energies) –geothermal site:.ca filetype:.pdf lang:.eng

Internet Research

Using Metasearch Engines

Until now each of your searches has used only a single search engine. Even with complex searching you only search one part of the Web at a time with a single search engine. If a single search engine doesn't deliver the number or quality of results you need, or if you would like to quickly compare results from different search engines to decide which one to use for a particular search, you may want to try a metasearch engine. **Metasearch engines** do not search the Web itself; rather they search other search engines' indexes. By searching more than one search engine's index simultaneously, metasearch engines often access more of the Web in a single search. However, metasearch engines usually do not search the best search engines, because of the fees such search engines charge. Also, search engines that are busy with too many other searches at the exact moment you conduct your search may be skipped, so results can be inconsistent. Table B-6 provides a sample list of metasearch engines and a description of their services. ▓▓▓▓ In the search process for information on alternative energy resources, you have become intrigued with geothermal energy. Jane suggests a simple search on this topic using a metasearch engine.

STEPS

QUICK TIP

No metasearch engine searches the entire Web. The metasearch engine's results are usually quite broad, but often not as deep as a single search engine's. A meta-search engine is a good place to start when you want to check the first few results from several search engines.

1. **Go to the Student Online Companion at** www.course.com/illustrated/research2, **click the** Ixquick link **(under "Metasearch engines")**
   The Ixquick Search page appears.

2. **Click the** Search text box, **type** "geothermal energy", **then click the** Search button
   Your search is now simultaneously sent to multiple search engines. Ixquick, along with ProFusion, is one of only a few "smart" metasearch engines, which translate search commands, like quotation marks, into queries that other search engines understand. If you cannot tell if the metasearch engine you are using does this, stick with very simple searches.

3. **Scroll through the results, noting the features of Ixquick's results: the** ranking stars, **the** Highlighted Result, **and the** list of search engines **after each result**
   Figure B-14 illustrates the Ixquick search results. Stars are used to rank the results by relevance. The Highlighted Result link takes you to a copy of the Web page that highlights your keywords for easy scanning. Ixquick also shows how each engine ranked pages and which results are sponsored.

QUICK TIP

The Highlighted Result is a copy of the Web page that Ixquick has made at its site. It is not the original. This copy can be useful if the original site is temporarily down.

4. **CScroll down, if necessary, then click the words** Highlighted Result
   This copy of the Web page highlights the keywords from your search query. This feature can help you quickly determine how useful the Web page might be.

5. **Use the Lesson 8 table in the Data File to record the number of matching results, save, print, and close the document, and exit your word-processing program**

Clues to use

Maximizing metasearching

To effectively use a metasearch engine, always read its Help pages. Help should let you know how "smart" the engine is in translating specific search commands into queries that other search engines understand. With this information, you know if you need to use quotation marks to indicate a phrase, or whether to use wildcards such as the asterisk or the question mark. If you're not sure how smart the metasearch engine is, use simple searches consisting of only a few keywords. Also, because the search engines used by a metasearch engine change regularly, note which engines are being used when you perform your search and which are returning the most useful results. Where a metasearch engine searches changes fairly often. You can usually find where one is currently searching by checking its Help pages or Advanced Search pages.

FIGURE B-14: Ixquick metasearch results

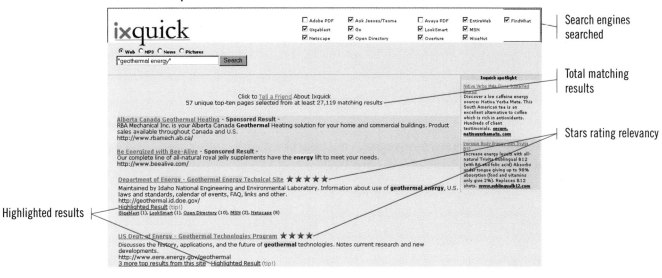

Search engines searched

Total matching results

Stars rating relevancy

Highlighted results

TABLE B-6: Metasearch engines

engine	where it searches	description
Dogpile	Google, AltaVista, Yahoo, Teoma, AskJeeves, About, LookSmart, FindWhat, Fast, and more	• Searches Web pages, news, images, audio, multimedia, directories, and shopping • Provides clickable topics for results • Results provided by relevance or by source
Fazzle	AltaVista, Yahoo, Teoma, MSN, Lycos, WiseNut, Netscape, LookSmart, OpenDirectory, and more	• Searches Web pages, downloads, audio, video, images, headline news, Canadian, international, government, entertainment, business, directories, encyclopedias, health, sports, and shopping • Results provided by relevance and are sortable
Ixquick	MSN, Teoma, Go, Wisenut, LookSmart, FindWhat, Netscape, Gigablast, EntireWeb, AskJeeves, OpenDirectory, and more	• Searches Web pages, news, images, and audio • Results provided as top hits from each engine • Translates and directs your query to search engines that can understand it • Marks results with stars to indicate rank in relevance • Provides result pages that highlight search terms
MetaCrawler	Google, AltaVista, Yahoo, About, FindWhat, LookSmart, AskJeeves, and more	• Searches Web pages, news, images, audio, multimedia, weather, directories, and shopping • Provides clickable topics for results • Results provided by relevance or source
Search.com	Google, LookSmart, Teoma, MSN, OpenDirectory, AskJeeves, Wisenut, Thunderstone, Yahoo, and more	• Searches Web pages, news, downloads, blogs, careers, directories, encyclopedias, audio, video, business, computers, law, health, medicine, quotes, shopping, and numerous other categories of sources by topic • Provides related clickable topics for results • Results provided by relevance or source and are sortable
Vivisimo	lii.org, MSN, Netscape, Lycos, LookSmart, eBay, FirstGov, and more	• Searches Web pages, news, images, sports, business, encyclopedia, government, and shopping • Provides clickable topics for results • Results provided by relevance or by source

Practice

▼ CONCEPTS REVIEW

Each of the following Venn diagrams represents searches. The dark color represents the search results. Write out the search for each diagram.

FIGURE B-15

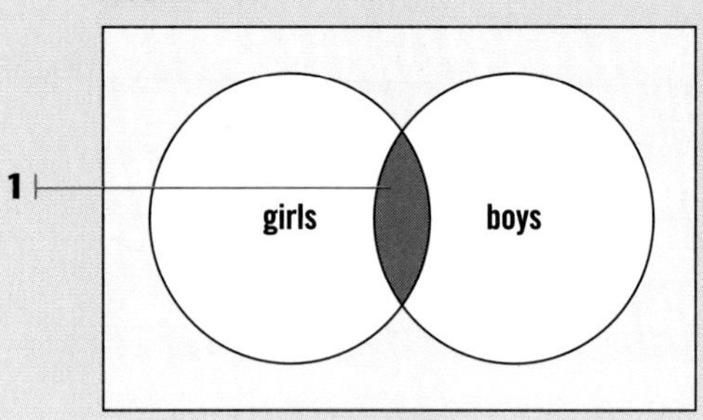

1 — girls boys

FIGURE B-16

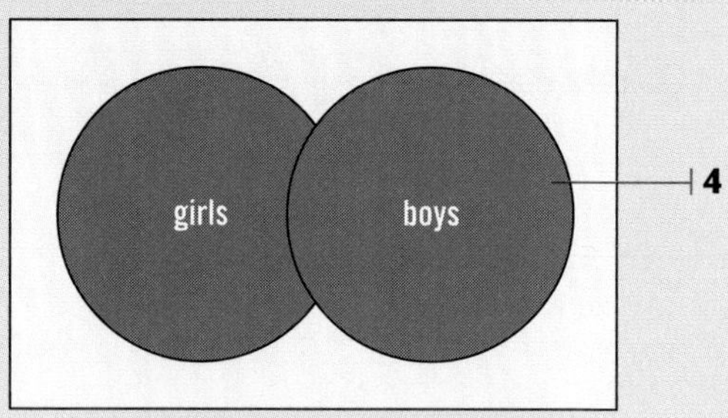

girls boys — 4

FIGURE B-17

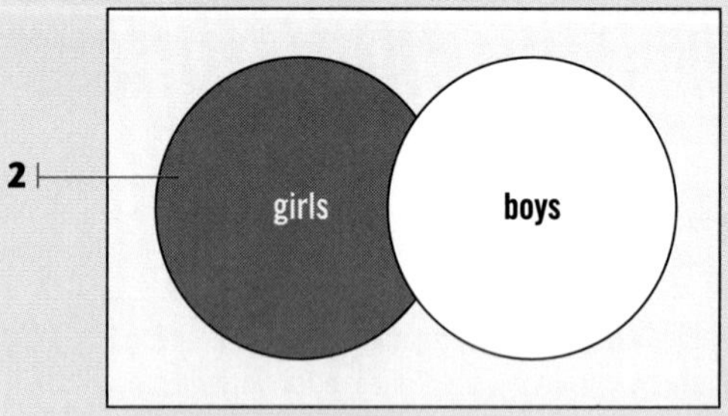

2 — girls boys

FIGURE B-18

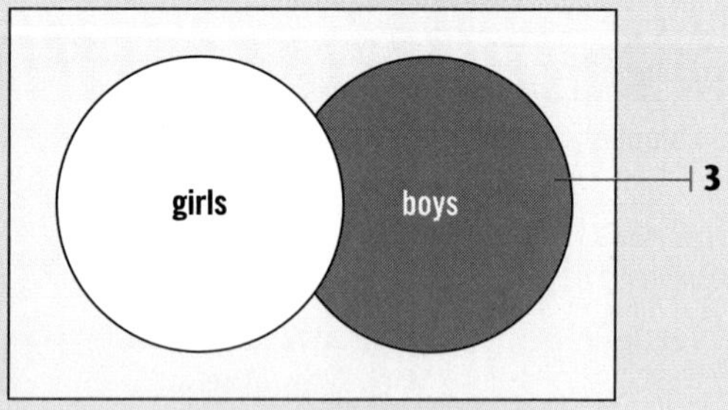

girls boys — 3

Match each term with the statement that best describes it.

5. **Boolean operators**   **a.** A way to visualize how Boolean operators work
6. **Venn diagrams**   **b.** Is used to connect synonyms
7. **AND operator**   **c.** A mathematical formula used by search engines to rank search results
8. **OR operator**   **d.** Aids to screen out unwanted Web pages
9. **AND NOT operator**   **e.** Force the order of operation in a Boolean search
10. **Metasearch engines**   **f.** Is used to exclude words from a search query
11. **Parentheses**   **g.** One way to narrow a search
12. **Filters**   **h.** Indicate how keywords are to relate to each other in a search query
13. **Algorithm**   **i.** A search engine that searches multiple search engines rather than the Web itself

Select the best answer from the following list of choices.

14. The place where two search result sets overlap is called the _____ of the two sets.
    a. Union
    b. Combination
    c. Intersection
    d. Margin

15. Each Boolean operator AND that links another keyword to your search, finds:
    a. More Web pages.
    b. Exactly the same number of Web pages.
    c. Fewer Web pages.
    d. None of the above.

16. Equivalent wording for the Boolean OR in an Advanced Search list box might be:
    a. Either of the words.
    b. All of the words.
    c. None of the words.
    d. Must not contain.

17. Which is *not* a standard variation of the Boolean operator AND NOT?
    a. NOT
    b. the hyphen or minus sign (–)
    c. NOT MORE
    d. ANDNOT

18. Which is *not* a potential downside to using metasearch engines?
    a. Instability
    b. Secrecy
    c. Inconsistency
    d. Usually limited to simple searches

19. If the order of operation in a complex Boolean search is not forced, the search tool:
    a. Reads the query from left to right.
    b. Inserts the parentheses for you.
    c. Returns no search results.
    d. Automatically applies filters to your search.

20. A search tool that doesn't recognize Boolean operators as English words in its basic search:
    a. Cannot be used to search with Boolean logic.
    b. Probably allows Boolean searching from text boxes or list boxes in its Advanced Search pages.
    c. Sometimes allows the Boolean AND and AND NOT if you use the plus sign (+) and the minus sign (–) instead of words.
    d. Both b and c are true.

21. The part of a URL that can contain a two-letter country code is the:
    a. File.
    b. File extension.
    c. Domain.
    d. Page.

22. Which is *not* true of all metasearch engines?

a. The search engines searched may change frequently.

b. They are a good place to start when you want to see the top results from several engines.

c. They interpret your search the way every other search engine can understand it.

d. They may skip searching an engine it normally searches if that engine is busy at that moment.

23. Using parentheses in a complex search tells the search engine that:

a. The part of the search inside the parentheses should be performed first.

b. The words inside the parentheses should be treated as a subset in the search.

c. The words inside the parentheses should be excluded from the search.

d. Both a and b are true.

▼ SKILLS REVIEW

1. Understand Boolean operators.

a. In your word-processing program, open the file called SR-UB.doc, save it as IR Skills Review-UB.doc, and add your name to the top of the page.

b. Use this file to describe the effects on search results of using each of the Boolean operators: AND, OR, and AND NOT.

2. Narrow the search with the AND operator.

a. Open your browser and go to the Student Online Companion at www.course.com/illustrated/research2, then click the Google link.

b. Perform an initial search on Mars.

c. Use the Skill #2 table in the Data File to record the number of search results.

d. Return to the Search page, edit your search by adding AND water.

e. Use the Skill #2 table in the Data File to record the number of search results.

f. Now edit your search again by adding AND robots.

g. Use the Skill #2 table in the Data File to record the number of search results, then save the document.

3. Expand the search with the OR operator.

a. Go to the Student Online Companion at www.course.com/illustrated/research2, then click the Google link.

b. Perform an initial search on Mars.

c. Use the Skill #3 table in the Data File to record the number of search results.

d. Return to the Search page, edit your search by adding OR water.

e. Use the Skill #3 table in the Data File to record the number of search results.

f. Now edit your search again by adding OR robots.

g. Use the Skill #3 table in the Data File to record the number of search results, then save the document.

4. Restrict a query with the AND NOT operator.

a. Go to the Student Online Companion at www.course.com/illustrated/research2, then click the Google link.

b. Perform an initial search on Mars.

c. Use the Skill #4 table in the Data File to record the number of search results.

d. Return to the Search page, edit your search by adding -water.

e. Use the Skill #4 table in the Data File to record the number of search results.

f. Now edit your AND NOT search again by adding -robots.

g. Use the Skill #4 table in the Data File to record the number of search results, then save the document.

5. Use multiple Boolean operators.

a. Go to the Student Online Companion at www.course.com/illustrated/research2, then click the Google link.

b. Perform an initial search on **Mars robots**.

c. Use the Skill #5 table in the Data File to record the number of search results.

d. Return to the Search page, edit your search by adding **(Europe OR Canada)** to the initial search criteria.

e. Use the Skill #5 table in the Data File to record the number of search results

6. Search with filters.

a. Go to the Student Online Companion at www.course.com/illustrated/research2, click the Google link, then click Advanced Search.

b. Perform an initial search on **Mars**.

c. Filter the results for **English**.

d. Use the Skill #6 table in the Data File to record the number of search results.

e. Return to the Search page, filter the search for Web pages updated in the **past year**, filter the domain for Germany (.da), then perform the search.

f. Use the Skill #6 table in the Data File to record the number of search results.

7. Combine Boolean operators and filters.

a. Go to the Student Online Companion at www.course.com/illustrated/research2, click the Google link, then click Advanced Search.

b. In the AND search text box, type **Mars**.

c. In the OR search text box, type **water geology**.

d. In the Language filter, select **English**, then click Search.

e. Use the Skill #7 table in the Data File to record the number of search results.

f. In the File Format filter, select **Microsoft PowerPoint**, and perform the search again.

g. Use the Skill #7 table in the Data File to record the number of search results.

8. Use a metasearch engine.

a. Go to the Student Online Companion at www.course.com/illustrated/research2, click the Ixquick link, then, if it is not already selected, select Web.

b. Perform an initial search on **Mars geology NASA**.

c. Use the Skill #8 table in the Data File to record the total number of matching results.

d. Look for Ixquick's statement about how many unique Web sites were searched. (*Hint*: You may need to scroll down the results page to find this information.) Use the Skill #8 table in the Data File to record the number of unique Web sites searched.

e. Use the Skill #8 table in the Data File to record the number of results on the first page of results that are marked for relevancy with three or more stars, then save the document.

▼ INDEPENDENT CHALLENGE 1

You want to find Web sites in Russia (domain .ru) about the Hermitage Museum. You don't read Russian so you want the Web pages to be in English.

    a. Use the Student Online Companion (www.course.com/illustrated/research2) to go to the Google site and open the Google Advanced Search page.

    b. Set the appropriate filters and perform your search.

    c. Print out the first page of Search results.

    d. Add your name to the top of the printout.

▼ INDEPENDENT CHALLENGE 2

You want to explain to a friend how Boolean operators work. You decide to draw a series of three Venn diagrams to illustrate what happens when using AND, OR, and AND NOT.

    a. Draw a Venn diagram illustrating how the AND operator works and label it "The AND operator."

    b. Draw a Venn diagram illustrating how the OR operator works and label it "The OR operator."

    c. Draw a Venn diagram illustrating how the AND NOT operator works and label it "The AND NOT operator."

    d. Add your name to the top of the page(s).

▼ INDEPENDENT CHALLENGE 3

Your history teacher told you that there is a connection between the Library of Congress and Thomas Jefferson. You decide to search the Internet to learn more about this connection.

    a. Use the Student Online Companion (www.course.com/illustrated/research2) to go to the AllTheWeb search engine.

    b. Click the Search text box, then type in two appropriate search phrases using quotation marks.

    c. Scroll through the first page of results and look for a URL with the clickable phrase **more hits from** beside it.

    d. Click this phrase by the link that you decide to check for your information.

    e. Print out the first page of results and add your name to the top of the page. (*Hint*: If AllTheWeb is not displaying this feature when you do your search, print out the first page of results from your original search.)

Advanced Challenge Exercise

You are curious about the highest-ranked results other search engines might return on your search for Thomas Jefferson and Library of Congress. Use a metasearch engine that translates your search to other search engines.

    ■ Use the Student Online Companion (www.course.com/illustrated/research2) to go to Ixquick. Click the Search text box, enter your search phrases, then click Search.

    ■ Print the first page of results, add your name at the top.

    ■ To learn more about how to search on Ixquick, click the link to the Help pages. (*Hint*: Because search engines redesign their pages frequently, you may have to look around the page for this link.)

    ■ In a text document, briefly describe two tips you learn from Ixquick's Help pages.

    ■ Save this document as **Unit B IC3-Advanced Challenge.doc**, add your name, print it, and attach it to your printout of the results page.

▼ INDEPENDENT CHALLENGE 4

You and some friends want to go on an ecologically friendly vacation—or an ecotour. You are interested in any North American destinations, but need the information to be in English.

a. Write your name on the top of a piece of paper, write out the topic and potential keywords, and circle the keywords and keyword phrases.

b. Write out your search strategy to make it easy to enter your query once you get online.
(*Hint*: You should use the Language filter and the search statement should look similar to this:
keyword +("*keyword* +keyword" OR *keyword* OR *keyword* OR "*keyword* +keyword")

c. Use the Student Online Companion (www.course.com/illustrated/research2) to go to Google's Advanced Search and perform the search.

d. Print out a copy of the first page of your search results, and write your name on the top of the page.

e. Attach the printout to the paper on which you wrote your topic and keywords.

Advanced Challenge Exercise

While looking over the results for an ecotour in North America, you become fascinated with the idea of a trip focusing on polar bears. You decide to restrict your search to find only relevant sites for this topic.

■ Return to Google's Advanced Search page and delete your previous search. Now search: (ecotour OR ecotourism) AND "polar bears" AND (Alaska OR Canada).

■ Print the first page of the search results and put your name at the top.

▼ VISUAL WORKSHOP

This Web page is the successful result of an effective search strategy. By following the steps below, recreate a search that can find this page.

a. Look at the Web page and choose some keywords that you might use to find this page. Write them down on a piece of paper.

b. On the same page, construct a search query that you think can find this Web page.

c. Go to an Internet search engine and perform your search. You may have to adjust your search as you go.

d. Once you find this Web page, print a copy and attach it to the paper on which you have written your query. (*Note*: If this page no longer exists on the Web, find one on the same subject.)

e. Add your name to the top of the paper.

FIGURE B-19

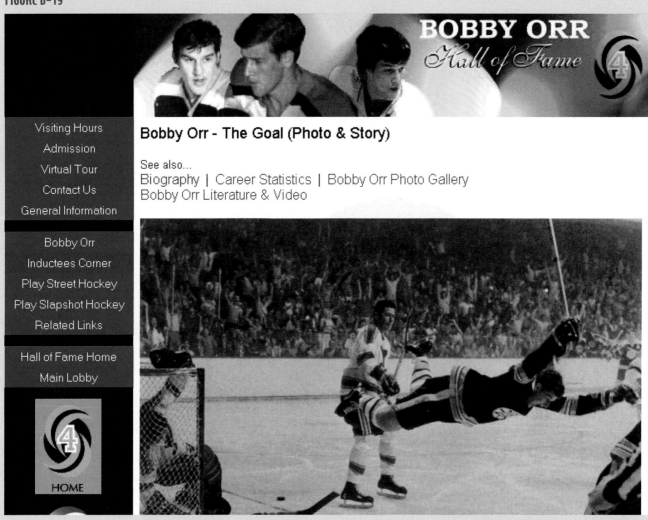

Browsing Subject Guides

OBJECTIVES

Understand subject guides
Browse a subject guide
Search a subject guide
Navigate a subject guide
Tap trailblazer pages
Use specialized search engines
Understand evaluative criteria
Evaluate Web pages

You have seen how a search of the Web can yield thousands, or even millions, of pages. Using Boolean operators in a planned search strategy to limit results can still leave you with more results than you can reasonably review. However, subject guides can help focus your search and are especially helpful when your knowledge of a topic is too limited for you to feel comfortable judging Web sites as you begin searching. A **subject guide** groups information by topic. These topics, typically arranged alphabetically and hierarchically, allow you to acquaint yourself with the breadth and/or depth of a subject. You navigate or browse a subject guide primarily by "**drilling down,**" or clicking through hierarchically arranged, increasingly specific subject headings. Many subject guides also allow keyword searching. Although subject guides are typically compiled by experts, rather than by software programs such as search engine spiders, you still need to know how to evaluate the sites gathered from a subject guide. The Portland City Planning team is overwhelmed with the number of Web sites you have found providing information on alternative energy sources. Now they want you to narrow the search and locate very specific information from reliable and credible sources. They particularly want you to focus on renewable energy, geothermal energy, and wind energy. Jane suggests you use subject guides for this phase of the research process.

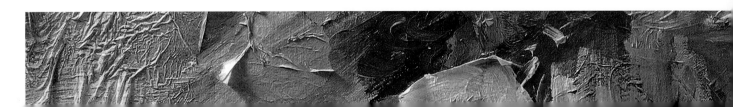

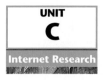
Understanding Subject Guides

Subject guides emphasize quality over quantity. Unlike search engines, subject guides are usually hand compiled and maintained by experts, offering users greater selectivity and quality of information, but less coverage than search engines. These experts often annotate the links to resources with useful information. Carefully designed selection criteria are used to select resources to include in subject guides, which are also known as **subject directories**, **Internet directories**, or **subject trees**. Subject guides organize the sites they index into hierarchical topics that you click your way down through to find relevant links. Links are arranged by subject, like books in a library, for easy access. Subject guides' content varies from general links to mostly commercial to mostly reference or academic links. Table C-1 provides more information about selected subject guides. ▓▓▓▓ You want to become more efficient at searching the Web for information on alternative energy. You decide to follow Jane's suggestion to learn more about subject guides.

DETAILS

Some notable characteristics of subject guides are:

- **Organization**

  Subject guides organize links to Web sites into topical hierarchies. A **hierarchy** is a ranked order. The ranked order typically goes from more general to more specific. For example, the general topics (in **bold**) in the lii.org (Librarians' Index to the Internet) subject guide, shown in Figure C-1, are followed by related, more specific topics. Clicking a topic, such as "Science," links to a list of subtopics. Subtopics link to increasingly more detailed topics. Clicking through topics and subtopics is called drilling down.

- **Selectivity and small size**

  Subject guides are selective. In better subject guides, qualified people rather than computer programs decide which Web pages are worthy of inclusion. Subject guides can provide links to useful sites that search engine spiders are unable to access. They often include **trailblazer pages** or Web pages with links to other sites covering all aspects of a topic. Subject experts also include sites that might cover one or two very detailed subtopics. This kind of selectivity ensures that returned Web pages are some of the best on the subject. However, because of this selectivity, subject guides are relatively small, which can be an advantage, saving you the time and trouble of sifting through thousands of search engine results.

- **Access methods**

  In addition to hierarchical lists of topics, better subject guides provide search forms with which you can use keywords to search their indexes. A local search engine allows you to search the titles and the annotations of indexed Web pages. A subject guide might also provide lists of topics arranged in various ways including alphabetically, geographically, chronologically, or by the Dewey Decimal subject classification system.

- **Annotations**

  Annotations are summaries or reviews of the contents of a Web page, written by the subject guide contributors, usually experts in the field, such as professionals or academics, or experts in information and the Web, such as librarians. Annotations of Web pages provided by subject guides make subject guides the tools of choice for many researchers.

- **Results display**

  Typical subject guide results include the number of results, annotations, and other subject terms under which sites are indexed. The latter can be especially useful when you are just learning about your topic and how it relates to other subjects. Figure C-2 shows a search results display on lii.org.

FIGURE C-1: lii.org home page (Librarians' Index to the Internet)

Search form

About link has information about the site

Help link provides guidelines on how to search

Click to open the Advanced Search page

Most general level of subjects/topics appear in **bold**

First level of subtopics

Special features on the site; might vary on your screen

FIGURE C-2: Result from lii.org subject guide

Your topic

Web site title

Web site URL

Annotation

Subject headings under which lii.org indexed this site

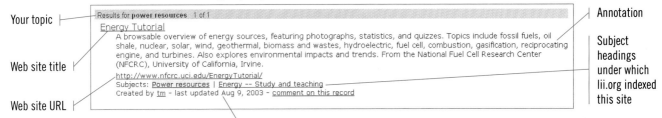

information on reviewer and the date site was reviewed

TABLE C-1: Sampling of guides (see the Student Online Companion at www.course.com/illustrated/research2)

subject guides	type/pages indexed	features
About.com	General, some academic/1 million+	Very broad, uneven quality, ads
BUBL LINK 5:15	Academic, scholarly/11,000+	Searchable, Dewey numbers, UK slant
EERE (Energy Efficiency and Renewable Energy)	Government, energy specific/600+ sites, 120,000 documents	Searchable, drill-down browsing
INFOMINE	Academic, scholarly, distributed/115,000+	Searchable, librarians, high quality
lii.org (Librarians' Index to the Internet)	General, reference/12,000+	Searchable, librarians, high quality
ipl (Internet Public Library)	General, reference/40,000	Very broad, Univ. of MI, librarians
LookSmart	Commercial/2.5 million	Searchable, mostly .coms
Open Directory Project	General/3 million	Accessed by most search engines, uneven
Scout Archives	Academic, reference/17,000	Searchable, high quality
WWW Virtual Library	Academic, general, distributed	Oldest on Web, volunteer indexers

Browsing a Subject Guide

Browsing is the easiest and most effective way to find information in a subject guide. The creators of subject guides review Web sites and organize links to them by topic. By clicking your way through the hierarchy of topics, from the most general to the most specific, you see what the guide's contributors deem the best Web sites. In a distributed subject guide, clicking categories can direct your browser to other sites. You decide to continue your search for information about alternative energy by browsing a few subject guides. Jane highly recommended lii.org (Librarians' Index to the Internet) so you begin there.

STEPS

1. **Open the Data File** IR-C1.doc **in a word-processing program, save it as** Subject Guides.doc, **open your browser, go to the Student Online Companion at** www.course.com/illustrated/research2, **and click the** lii.org link **(under "Subject guides")**

   Lii.org (Librarians' Index to the Internet) appears. Notice there is a search form as well as headings you can click to view broad subject categories. You decide that your topic, "*alternative energy*," might be under the heading "Science, Technology, & Computers."

> **QUICK TIP**
>
> Topics in bold lead to subtopics.

2. **Click the** Science, Technology, & Computers link

   The resulting page, as shown in Figure C-3, offers more categories.

> **QUICK TIP**
>
> A subject guide's list of topics offers numerous choices. If the one that seems most relevant doesn't lead to what you need, or to explore other topics, click your browser's Back button.

3. **Click the** All Science Topics link **to view the entire list of Science subtopics**

   The Science subtopics are displayed. Again you have to make a choice. There are several categories you would like to explore, but you decide to pick *Environment* first.

4. **Click the** Environment link

   The next level of subtopics is displayed. Several might be useful, including "Energy Conservation," "Environmental Responsibility," "Fuel Cells," "Solar Energy," "Sustainable Development," and "Wind Power." You decide to start with "Renewable Energy."

5. **Click the** Renewable Energy link, **select a Web site, then record the URL in the Lesson 2 table in the Data File**

   Figure C-4 shows sites indexed with the phrase "*renewable energy*." This page is the equivalent of a search engine's results page. Notice the results highlight this phrase. Next you decide to explore a distributed subject guide.

> **QUICK TIP**
>
> If you had entered "*renewable energy*" in the home page search form, this would have been your results page. If you are unsure of keywords, a subject guide is a good starting place and will help you identify effective keywords.

6. **Go to the** Student Online Companion, **then click the** WWW Virtual Library link **(under "Subject guides")**

   Again the subject guide's home page provides subject categories you can navigate. You decide to try "Engineering."

7. **Click the** Engineering link, **look over more topics, then click the** Chemical Engineering link

   This page is clearly different from the last few pages you viewed. Look at the URL in your browser's address bar—you are no longer at WWW Virtual Library. You have been directed to another site.

8. **Locate and click** Energy, Conservation and Efficiency **to see a list of annotated links, record the title of one of the sites in the Lesson 2 table in the Data File, then save the Data File**

FIGURE C-3: lii.org Science, Technology, & Computers page

Main topic selected from home page

Headings for first level of subtopics

Librarians' Index to the Internet
lii.org
Information You Can Trust

>> Home
>> About
>> Subscribe
>> Help
>> Suggest a Site
>> Comments
>> More Search Tools

[   ] [SEARCH LII.ORG] Advanced Search

Science, Technology, & Computers

All Science Topics

Popular Fields:

Headings for second level of subtopics

- Agriculture
- Animals
- Anthropology
- Archaeology
- Astronomy
- Biology
- Chemistry
- Earth Sciences

All Technology Topics

Popular Topics:

- Artificial Intelligence
- Automobiles
- Aviation
- Computers
- Engineering
- Internet
- Inventions & Inventors
- Lighthouses

Related topics

Related Topics:

- Dictionaries
- Health & Medicine
- Mathematics
- Museums
- Science Projects
- Scientists
- Time
- Weather

FIGURE C-4: lii.org results: "renewable energy"

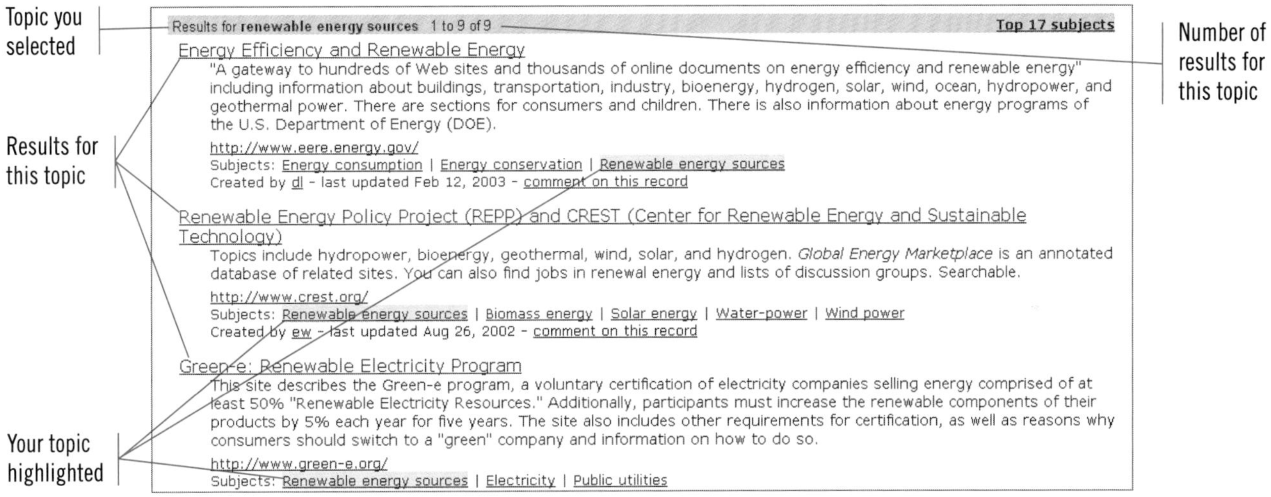

Topic you selected

Results for **renewable energy sources** 1 to 9 of 9

Top 17 subjects

Number of results for this topic

Energy Efficiency and Renewable Energy
"A gateway to hundreds of Web sites and thousands of online documents on energy efficiency and renewable energy" including information about buildings, transportation, industry, bioenergy, hydrogen, solar, wind, ocean, hydropower, and geothermal power. There are sections for consumers and children. There is also information about energy programs of the U.S. Department of Energy (DOE).
http://www.eere.energy.gov/
Subjects: Energy consumption | Energy conservation | Renewable energy sources
Created by dl - last updated Feb 12, 2003 - comment on this record

Results for this topic

Renewable Energy Policy Project (REPP) and CREST (Center for Renewable Energy and Sustainable Technology)
Topics include hydropower, bioenergy, geothermal, wind, solar, and hydrogen. *Global Energy Marketplace* is an annotated database of related sites. You can also find jobs in renewal energy and lists of discussion groups. Searchable.
http://www.crest.org/
Subjects: Renewable energy sources | Biomass energy | Solar energy | Water-power | Wind power
Created by ew - last updated Aug 26, 2002 - comment on this record

Green-e: Renewable Electricity Program
This site describes the Green-e program, a voluntary certification of electricity companies selling energy comprised of at least 50% "Renewable Electricity Resources." Additionally, participants must increase the renewable components of their products by 5% each year for five years. The site also includes other requirements for certification, as well as reasons why consumers should switch to a "green" company and information on how to do so.
http://www.green-e.org/
Subjects: Renewable energy sources | Electricity | Public utilities

Your topic highlighted

Clues to Use

Distributed subject guides

WWW Virtual Library and the Open Directory Project are examples of distributed subject guides. **Distributed subject guides** are created by a variety of contributors working somewhat independently. Each group or person is usually responsible for a subtopic of a main topic. These guides are said to be "distributed" because rather than being on a subject guide's computer, the Web pages for different parts of the guide are stored on different computers, distributed around the country or around the world. Because distributed subject guides have many contributors working independently, each with varying levels of expertise and resources, distributed subject guides tend to have an uneven quality and a lack of standardization. However, this potential downside is balanced by the fact that these different parts of the guide's index are often maintained by subject experts with a high level of awareness of what is available on the Web in their field.

Searching a Subject Guide

Each subject guide has a unique way of organizing information. As you saw in the last lesson, "Energy" might appear under "Science" at one guide and under "Engineering" at another. Some subject guides also offer their own local search engine to provide a more direct approach to finding information. Like a regular Web search engine, a subject guides' local search engine searches its own indexes to return results. The difference is, unlike a Web search engine whose spiders constantly crawl the Web adding the full text of pages to its indexes, a subject guide's index contains only the annotations, keywords, and subject headings assigned to the selected Web pages by the guide's contributors and editors. You want to find more Web sites on geothermal energy. From a list of subject guides Jane gave you, you decide to try Open Directory and LookSmart next.

STEPS

1. **Go to the Student Online Companion at www.course.com/illustrated/research2, click the LookSmart link (under "Subject guides") to open the LookSmart home page, type geothermal in the Search text box, then click the Search button**

   LookSmart's results appear, as shown in Figure C-5. Notice the first set of results are sponsored sites, or sites which have paid for placement in the results. Below the returned results, you have the option of clicking links to more sites on related categories. You decide to follow the directory category "Geothermal Energy."

QUICK TIP

Remember that Web sites redesign their pages frequently. If you don't see an element mentioned in the steps look around the page for a similarly labeled element.

2. **Click the Geothermal Energy link (under "Related Directory Categories"), look over the annotations, select a site, then record its title in the Lesson 3 table in the Data File**

   Notice that at the top of the page you see "You are here" followed by a directory path: Home > Work & Money > Industries > Energy & Utilities > Energy by Type > Renewable Energy > Geothermal. This shows you where you are in the directory. If instead of searching, you had clicked "Work & Money" on the home page, and continued to drill down along this path, you would have ended up on this page. Now you want to search Open Directory, another subject guide that provides a local search engine.

3. **Go to the Student Online Companion, click the Open Directory link (under "Subject guides")**

   Figure C-6 shows the Open Directory's home page. Now you will perform a search.

4. **Type geothermal in the Search text box, click the Search button, look over the annotations, choose a site, then record its title in the Lesson 3 table in the Data File**

   The results of the search include a list of Open Directory categories showing possible directory paths for further searching. You decide to drill down by clicking one of these paths.

5. **Click the Science: Technology: Energy: Geothermal link, look over the annotations, select a site, record its title in the Lesson 3 table in the Data File, then save the Data File**

FIGURE C-5: LookSmart search: *geothermal*

Search form

Sponsored results

Search results

Click these tabs to search the Web or indexed articles

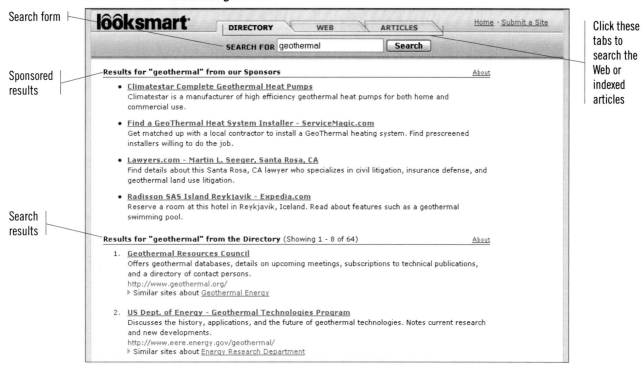

FIGURE C-6: Open Directory home page

Search form

Subject category topics (**bold**)

Subtopics

Click this link for an advanced search

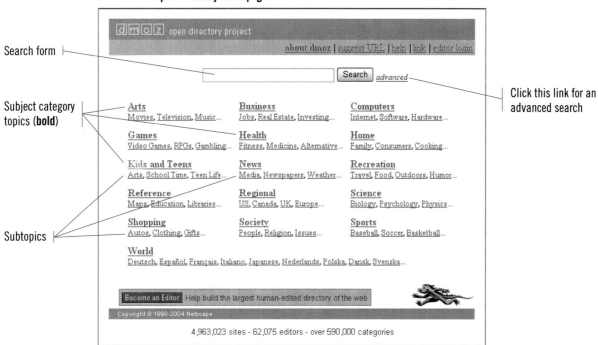

Navigating a Subject Guide

Subject guides may provide hierarchical lists of topics, local search engines, geographical lists, alphabetical lists, or other ways to access the pages in their database. BUBL LINK / 5:15 (BUBL—pronounced *bubble*) also indexes by the Dewey Decimal system, the same numeric subject classification system used in many libraries. Jane mentions this interesting feature in BUBL and you decide to try it.

STEPS

QUICK TIP

Look at BUBL's URL and note the domain. The .uk domain indicates this site is from the United Kingdom. BUBL has an interesting name. For more information on its meaning, click the About link on the home page.

1. **Go to the Student Online Companion at** www.course.com/illustrated/research2**, then click the BUBL LINK / 5:15 link (under "Subject guides")**

   The BUBL home page appears, as shown in Figure C-7. You immediately see there are several ways to search this subject guide, including Subject Menus, A-Z, Dewey, Countries, Types, and by clicking the broad subject headings. You decide to explore a few of these options.

2. **Click the Subject Menus link at the top of the page, look over the list of subjects, then click the Energy link**

   The alphabetical list of topics under Subject Menus is a way to start clicking through subjects from a more comprehensive list than the broad headings on the home page. The subtopics under "Energy" include their corresponding Dewey Decimal numbers. You decide to click a Dewey number.

QUICK TIP

You can use the descriptions at BUBL to help you determine the authority of a site. If you want further information about an author, search on his or her name.

3. **Click the 333.79 Renewable energy link**

   A list of Web sites indexed at BUBL under "333.79 Renewable energy" appears. BUBL provides useful information, including site authors. Now you decide to try the alphabetical index.

4. **Click the A-Z link at the top of the page, click the R link, then click the Renewable energy link**

   The list of Web sites related to renewable energy appears, as shown in Figure C-8. BUBL displays the results two ways: on the left side for easy previewing, BUBL lists the titles, as links, of the Web pages indexed under the term "Renewable energy." To the right, BUBL lists the titles, as well as their annotations and other information, such as their corresponding Dewey numbers. Now you want to try searching by Dewey number.

5. **Near the top of the page, click the Dewey link**

   Figure C-9 shows the Dewey class. You want to look for 333.79 because you learned from your previous searches that this is the Dewey number for the renewable energy topics.

QUICK TIP

This exercise can also provide you with background on how books on your topic might be cataloged in your library.

6. **Click the 300 Social sciences link, on the next page click the 330 Economics link, then click the 333 Environment and economics of land and energy link**

   This page should look familiar. In fact, you reached the same page earlier in Step 2 when you searched the guide using the Subject menus.

7. **Click the 333.79 Renewable energy link, select one site, record its title in the Lesson 4 table in the Data File, then save the Data File**

   This page should also look familiar. This is the same list you found in Step 3 above.

FIGURE C-7: BUBL LINK / 5:15 home page

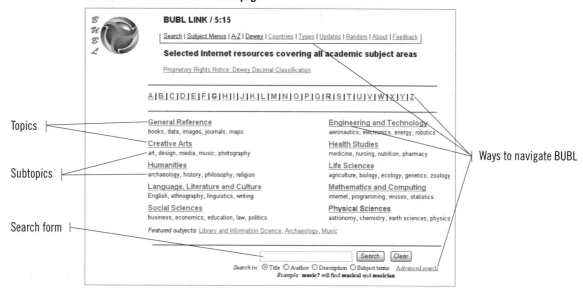

Topics

Subtopics

Search form

Ways to navigate BUBL

FIGURE C-8: BUBL result: "renewable energy"

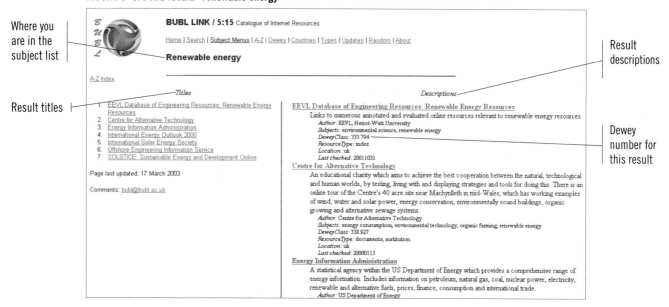

Where you are in the subject list

Result titles

Result descriptions

Dewey number for this result

FIGURE C-9: BUBL Browse by Dewey Class page

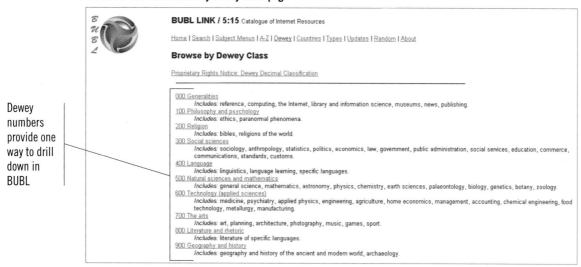

Dewey numbers provide one way to drill down in BUBL

Tapping Trailblazer Pages

Trailblazer pages are created by scholars, experts, and organizations who seek to organize and provide links to better Web sites in their field. They are an excellent source of reliable Web resources. These pages may be narrow or broad in scope, but all attempt to provide thorough coverage of their subject. A good trailblazer page not only provides links to useful sites, it also provides a logical, well-organized way of navigating them. Organizational features may include a local search engine, user-friendly navigation throughout the site, and a **site map** (an index to the pages on the site). ▰▰▰ To maximize use of trailblazer pages, you want to familiarize yourself with them. Jane recommends the U.S. Department of Energy's Energy Efficiency and Renewable Energy site (EERE) as a gold mine of information. You decide to explore it.

STEPS

TROUBLE

The EERE Web site on your screen might look different. Many Web sites change appearance over time. Usually the information remains the same; however, you might need to locate and click slightly different links to find it.

1. **Go to the Student Online Companion at www.course.com/illustrated/research2, then click the EERE link (under "Subject guides")**

   The EERE site appears as shown in Figure C-10. This site links to over 600 other sites and contains over 120,000 documents at the EERE site itself. Look around the home page, then look for a link that reads "Site Map."

2. **Click the Site Map link, then explore this page**

   The site map provides links to access all parts of the site. You want to see a more comprehensive listing of the EERE's Web site links.

3. **Click the Alphabetical Listing of Sites link**

   An alphabetized list of the sites linked from the EERE site appears.

4. **Look over the page and range of links, then scroll back to the top and click the Home link**

   The EERE home page reappears. You want to see how the subtopics are organized.

5. **Click the Bioenergy link under Renewable Energy**

   EERE's Bioenergy page appears, as shown in Figure C-11. After scanning this page, you want to see if there is any information about your city, Portland, Oregon.

QUICK TIP

Whenever you find a great site such as EERE, that you know you will want to reference again, save it as an Internet Explorer Favorite or a Netscape Bookmark.

6. **In the Search text box, type "Portland Oregon", then click the Search button**

   Figure C-12 shows your search results. You notice the number of search results and conclude EERE is a gold mine of Web resources.

7. **Look over your results, select one site, record its title in the Lesson 5 table in the Data File, then save the Data File**

FIGURE C-10: EERE home page

Search form

Site map

Topics and subtopics

FIGURE C-11: EERE Bioenergy page

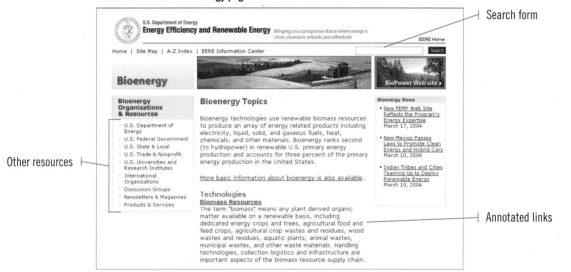

Search form

Other resources

Annotated links

FIGURE C-12: EERE search: "Portland Oregon"

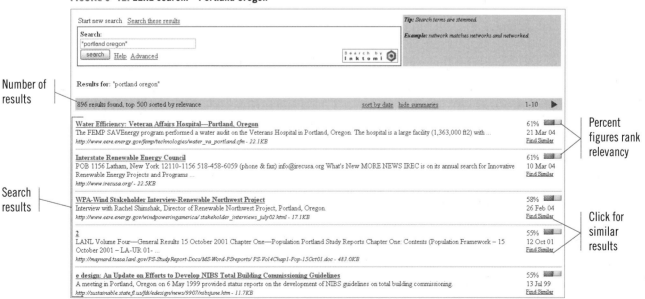

Number of results

Search results

Percent figures rank relevancy

Click for similar results

Using Specialized Search Engines

Search engines often find too many results and subject guides may provide fewer than you need. Specialized search engines can combine the best features of both. **Specialized search engines** act similarly to regular Web search engines, except, like some subject guides, they limit the Web pages they search by subject. Specialized search engines are available for a wide variety of topics, including law, medicine, computers, and energy. Jane mentions that the specialized search engine, Source for Renewable Energy, is a good place to locate alternative energy resources on the Web. You decide to see if you can find out who sells wind energy equipment in Portland.

STEPS

1. **Go to the Student Online Companion at www.course.com/illustrated/research2, click The Source for Renewable Energy link (under "Specialized search engines")**
   The Source for Renewable Energy appears, as shown in Figure C-13. As in other subject guides there are multiple ways to search, but you want to explore the specialized search engine.

2. **Click the Search the Business Guide link to open the site's specialized search engine**

3. **In the Search text box, type "wind energy" "Portland Oregon", then click the Search button**
   Make sure to type the two keyword phrases in two separate sets of quotation marks. This guarantees that the search engine interprets your search correctly. Your results page should look familiar—Google provides the search technology for this site. Figure C-14 shows the results page.

4. **Scroll through the results and notice that each link's URL begins with "energy.sourceguides.com," select one of the links, look for products, services, and contact information, then record the URL for this link in the Lesson 6 table in the Data File**
   The fact that each link's URL begins with the same domain indicates that you only searched this specialized site, not the Web. Now you decide to try accessing this information another way.

5. **Click the Source guides icon at the top of the results page to open the Source For Renewable Energy home page, click the geographic location link, click the United States icon, click the by State icon, click the Oregon link, click the by Product Type icon, then click the Wind Energy Products link**
   This is the drill-down method of searching a subject guide. Look at the path you used under the Source Guides icon at the top of the page. Figure C-15 illustrates your results page.

6. **Look over the results, select one that has its own Web page, record the URL in the Lesson 6 table in the Data File, then save the Data File**

Clues to Use

How do you find a specialized search engine?

Ask a librarian or instructor to recommend a specialized search engine for your research topic. They may also be able to help you identify lists of trailblazer pages, which are good sources of important Web sites in subject areas, such as the ones listed in the Student Online Companion under the heading "Specialized search engines."

FIGURE C-13: The Source for Renewable Energy home page

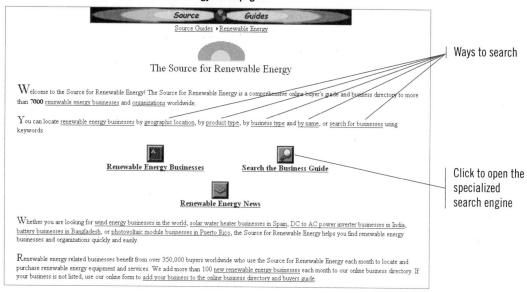

Ways to search

Click to open the specialized search engine

FIGURE C-14: The Source for Renewable Energy search: "wind energy" "Portland Oregon"

Your search

Search results

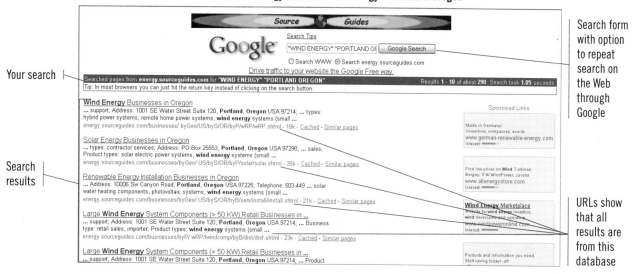

Search form with option to repeat search on the Web through Google

URLs show that all results are from this database

FIGURE C-15: The Source for Renewable Energy drill-down results

Your topic

Annotation for first search result

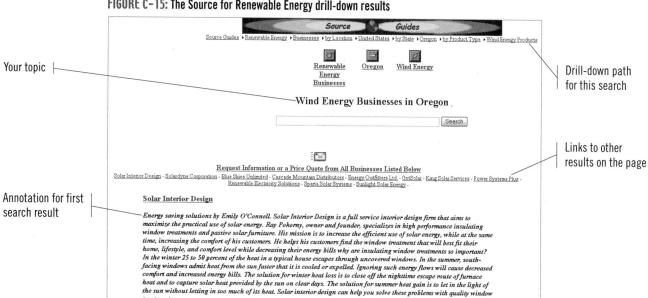

Drill-down path for this search

Links to other results on the page

Understanding Evaluative Criteria

Evaluative criteria are standards used to determine if a Web site is appropriate for your needs. No matter what your subject or which search tool you use, resources you find must be evaluated. Web information can go directly from the author to you, with no intervening editorial or review process used for most printed material, requiring you to be more critical. In an earlier unit you practiced evaluating search results to choose which pages to explore. After exploring sites that passed your search results evaluation, you will have eliminated some and kept others. Now the latter ones must pass through another level of assessment. Figure C-16 illustrates the criteria you should use in determining if a site is appropriate. Figure C-17 shows an example of identifying evaluative criteria on a Web page. You have found so many sites on your subject that you are concerned about selecting the best ones to present to the team at the City Planning Office. Jane provides you with criteria to use to evaluate Web pages to determine which pages are appropriate for your needs.

DETAILS

The list of criteria include:

- **Organization**

  The way a Web site is organized is often almost as important as its content. Great content on a page can be defeated by poor design and functionality. Attractiveness and graphic features can mask a lack of meaningful content. Answer these questions as you evaluate a page:
  - Is the site well designed and functional? Is there a site map and Help page?
  - Is it easy to navigate? Do the navigational buttons and internal links work?
  - Is it searchable? Are there a variety of ways to access material?

QUICK TIP

If there is an e-mail link for the author or creator, feel free to write and ask questions.

- **Authority**

  Knowing the author's name and qualifications is key to determining how credible or reliable the material is. Try a search for the author to see if he or she has written in the field. Consider these questions:
  - Is the author identified? Are the author's qualifications identified? Are resources documented?
  - Is there contact information for the author? Are other publications by the author listed?
  - Is the author associated with a university, a government agency, or an organization?

QUICK TIP

Is there a bibliography or are resources well documented?

- **Objectivity and Accuracy**

  A site's objectivity and accuracy greatly affects its appropriateness. Nothing is wrong with selling a product or advocating an idea, but that should be stated as the purpose of the page. You need to validate the site's objectivity and accuracy by looking at other online or printed information on the topic. Consider these questions:
  - Does the author state the purpose of the site? Is the content presented as fact or as opinion?
  - Is the publisher, sponsor, or host for the site identified?
  - What do other Web sites or articles say about the author or sponsor?

- **Scope**

  The **scope** of a site is the range of topics it covers. Consider these questions:
  - Is there an introduction or other information explaining the scope of the site?
  - Who is the intended audience? Is it useful for professionals? Lay people? Students?
  - Does the scope of the site match your needs?

QUICK TIP

You may need to go to the site's home page or About page to look for dates.

- **Currency**

  Currency or timeliness may or may not be an issue for your search. Consider these questions:
  - Is there a creation or revision date?
  - Are there many broken links? If so, this may indicate the site is not being updated or maintained.
  - Does the currency of the site match your needs?

FIGURE C-16: Evaluative criteria for determining if a site is appropriate for your needs

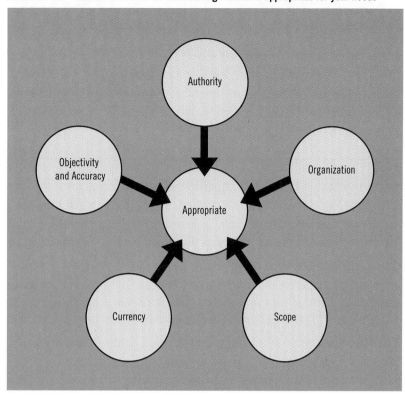

FIGURE C-17: Identifying evaluative criteria on a Web page

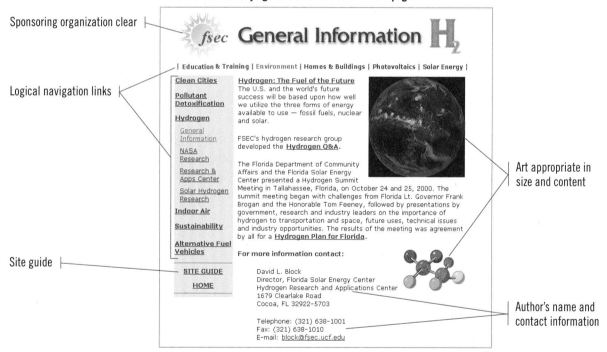

Clues to Use

Are there any objective Web pages?

No Web page is totally objective. Commercial sites (.com) usually exist to sell something. Nonprofit organizations (.org) usually have strong opinions about their causes. Even an educational page (.edu) may be affected by its creator's views. Ideally, these sites divulge their positions openly, but very often you may have to dig around to find out. Educational (.edu) and government (.gov) sites generally are more objective, or at least support their ideas with documented facts. As long as you can ascertain a page's bias, you can come to your own conclusions about its content.

Evaluating Web Pages

Every time you use a search engine or a subject guide, you must choose which Web sites to include in your research. The evaluative criteria in the last lesson are tools that can enable you to quickly eliminate the least useful sites so that you can focus your time and energy on the most relevant ones. ▰▰▰ You have located a site about geothermal data. You think it may be relevant to your search but need to evaluate it more closely. You use the criteria Jane gave you earlier.

STEPS

TROUBLE

If the Geothermal Data site has moved or disappeared from the Web, the Student Online Companion will link to a new site and provide new directions to follow.

1. **Go to the Student Online Companion at www.course.com/illustrated/research2, then click the Geothermal Data link (under "Specialized search engines")**

   Figure C-18 illustrates the top of the page entitled "Virginia Tech Geothermal Data WWW Home Page." Figure C-19 illustrates the bottom of that page.

2. **Scroll through the Web page**

   As you scan the page, you realize the level of writing and its scope are of interest to you. The titles of the topics indicate that it links to some very practical information. You notice the link to Virginia Polytechnic Institute & State University in the first paragraph and decide to follow it in order to learn more about the host of this site.

3. **Click the Virginia and Polytechnic Institute & State University link**

   The Virginia Tech home page appears. You have now verified that the sponsor of the site is a university in Virginia and are satisfied that it is a reputable organization. Now you are interested in the author.

4. **Click the Back button in your browser to return to the original Web page, then click the author's name John K. Costain near the bottom of the page**

   The author's home page should appear, as in Figure C-20. Scrolling through this page you notice some impressive accomplishments. The author has provided information about his research and classes he has taught. You decide to read a bit more about the author in his *vita*, a word used in the education field to refer to a biographical sketch and list of experience, similar to a resume.

5. **Click the Vita link, then scroll through the author's vita**

   The author's credentials impress you. You want to see how up to date the Web page is.

6. **Click the Back button in your browser to return to the original Web page, click the Research link, then scroll the page for a revision date**

   You notice a date at the bottom of the page that is recent enough for your needs.

7. **Find an e-mail address for the author, then record the address in the Lesson 8 table in the Data File**

8. **Type your name at the top of the Data File, save, print, and close the Data File, then close your word-processing program**

FIGURE C-18: Virginia Tech Geothermal Data: top of home page

Page title

Virginia Tech Geothermal Data WWW Home Page

About the
page

SAGE -- Summer of Applied Geophysical Experience

Link to
hosting
institution

Welcome to the WWW home page for southeastern United States Geothermal Data at the Regional Geophysics Laboratory in the Department of Geological Sciences at Virginia Polytechnic Institute & State University. Development of this site was funded primarily by the Department of Energy under Agreement Number DE-FG07-96ID13454 to Virginia Tech. The site is useful for those interested in terrestrial heat flow, practical applications of low-temperature geothermal energy, and also provides an excellent temperature versus depth data base for those wanting to do their own calculations to evaluate hypotheses of global warming using a geothermal approach to climate reconstruction. This site is frequently updated to include temperature data from hundreds of temperature and other geophysical logs, rock thermal conductivity, and heat flow values from New Jersey to Georgia. Datasets can be displayed and/or downloaded for use by the user. Clicking on the items below will provide information on the data available. To browse this page correctly we suggest that you get a copy of the Microsoft Internet Explorer or the Netscape Navigator.

Heat contained within the Earth that can be recovered and put to useful work is called geothermal energy. The heat energy is contained in normal occurrences of subsurface groundwater, which is transported to the surface of the earth by pumping. Low- to moderate-temperature (20°C to 150°C [68°F to 302°F]) geothermal resources in the United States are widespread and are used to provide direct heat for homes and industry. High-temperature (above 150°C [302°F]) geothermal resources in the United States, present primarily in the west, are used in electric power generation. And, throughout the country, the stable temperature of the ground just below the surface can be used by geothermal heat pumps to both heat and cool buildings (geothermal energy). The low- to moderate-temperature geothermal resources constitute an important renewable non-electric power energy resource that is just beginning to be utilized in the eastern United States to heat and cool buildings. As these space-heating applications grow in popularity to include entire residential and industrial complexes

---

FIGURE C-19: Virginia Tech Geothermal Data: bottom of home page

Hot Springs in the Southeastern United States

Temperatures at the Base of the Atlantic Coastal Plain Sediments

Evidence from Precision Temperature logs for Deep Fracture Permeability in Crystalline Rocks in the Eastern and Southeastern United States

Related Links

DOE Final Technical Report for Agreement Number DE-FG07-96ID13454

E-mail
contact for
author

Regional Geophysics Laboratory, Department of Geological Sciences, Virginia Polytechnic Institute and State University
Comments about this web site to: costain@vt.edu
This geothermal web site can be accessed using either of the following URLs.
http://geothermal.geol.vt.edu
http://rglsun1.geol.vt.edu
Last updated: 03/26/03

Last revision
date for the
home page

Author of
the page

John K. Costain
Department of Geological Sciences
1046 Derring Hall, Blacksburg, VA 24061-0422

FIGURE C-20: John K. Costain's home page

John K. Costain: Professor Emeritus of Geophysics

Office: 1050 Derring Hall
Phone: (540) 231-8912 **Fax:** (540) 231-3386

Practice

CONCEPTS REVIEW

Label each of the parts of the following subject guide.

FIGURE C-21

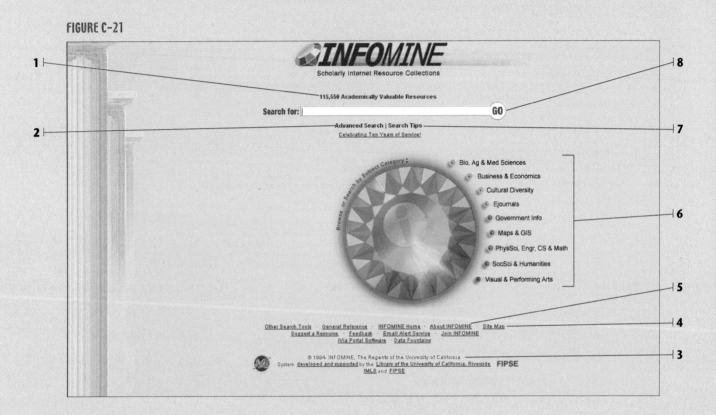

Match each term with the statement that best describes it.

9. **Hierarchy**

10. **Trailblazer pages**

11. **Annotation**

12. **Drill down**

13. **Dewey Decimal**

14. **Site map**

15. **Specialized search engine**

16. **Evaluative criteria**

17. **Distributed**

a. A carefully written summary or review

b. Refers to clicking through topics to reach links on a results page

c. Standards that help you determine if a Web site is right for your needs

d. Often indexed in subject guides, these pages link to valuable sites, usually subject specific

e. Refers to a subject guide compiled by numerous editors and stored on numerous computers

f. Combines some of the best features of both a subject guide and a search engine

g. A stratified or ranked order

h. Subject classification system used by many libraries and some subject guides

i. An index to a Web site

Select the best answer from the list of choices.

18. Traits that all subject guides share are:
   a. They are organized hierarchically and are selective in the Web sites they list.
   b. They are relatively small compared to search engines.
   c. They include annotations to the Web sites.
   d. All of the above.

19. One definition of *browsing* is:
   a. Clicking through the hierarchy of topics at a subject guide.
   b. Using a local search engine to search a subject guide.
   c. Using criteria to evaluate a Web site.
   d. Finding out who wrote a Web page.

20. A distributed subject guide:
   a. Is maintained by one editor.
   b. Usually resides on only one computer.
   c. Is the same thing as a search engine.
   d. May lack standardization.

21. An annotated subject guide:
   a. Allows you to write reviews of Web sites.
   b. Contains reviews of Web sites.
   c. Reviews other subject guides.
   d. Allows you to search for reviews of search engines.

22. A local search engine:
   a. Is best searched with complex Boolean queries.
   b. Does not usually exist at a subject guide.
   c. Searches only in one city or state.
   d. Is best searched using one keyword or short phrase.

23. Which is *not* a way subject guides are organized?
   a. Alphabetically
   b. By hexadecimal
   c. By Dewey Decimal
   d. Topically

24. Specialized search engines:
   a. Only exist on a few topics.
   b. Are like a regular search engine except they index far more Web pages.
   c. Cannot be queried using Boolean operators.
   d. Share qualities of both subject guides and search engines.

25. Which is a common way to find a specialized search engine?
   a. Ask a librarian or professor.
   b. See if there is a link to one from a trailblazer page.
   c. Visit a collection of specialized search engines on the Web.
   d. All of the above.

26. When evaluating a Web page to determine its authority, you do *not*:
   a. Consider the qualifications of the author of a Web page.
   b. Consider the conviction with which an author writes.
   c. Look to see what else the author has written.
   d. Look to see if resources are well documented.

▼ SKILLS REVIEW

1. Understand subject guides.

   a. Open the Data File called **SR-UC.doc**, save it as **IR Skills Review-UC.doc**, and enter your name in the space provided.

   b. Choose at least three of the five common traits of subject guides mentioned in Lesson 1.

   c. In the Skill #1 table in the Data File write a few sentences about how these traits make subject guides useful for Web research and different from search engines.

   d. Save the Data File.

2. Browse a subject guide.

   a. A friend is interested in changing careers and asks you to help her find information on companies offering good opportunities for a working mother.

   b. Open your browser and go to the Student Online Companion at www.course.com/illustrated/research2.

   c. Click the lii.org link under Subject guides.

   d. Look over the general topics and click the one that mentions jobs.

   e. In the resulting subtopics, click Career Development.

   f. Scroll down looking through these results. When you find one with an additional subject heading for **Women—Employment**, click that subject link.

   g. Look over these Web site links and annotations and pick one to share with your friend.

   h. In the Skill #2 table in the Data File, record the title and the URL of the Web site you selected, then save the Data File.

3. Search a subject guide.

   a. You are writing a book and want to avoid plagiarizing the information you read.

   b. Go to the Student Online Companion and click the INFOMINE link.

   c. In the Search text box, type **plagiarism**.

   d. In the Skill #3 table in the Data File, record how many relevant Web sites are listed.

   e. Follow a link that you think would be a good one to use.

   f. In the Skill #3 table in the Data File, record the title and URL, then save the Data File.

4. Navigate a subject guide.

   a. Your younger brother is writing a report for his high school Social Studies class about families in Canada. He has one statistics book with some good information in it, but would like more. You notice the book has the Dewey number 310 on it. You decide to look in BUBL using the Dewey number for more information.

   b. Go to the Student Online Companion and click the BUBL LINK / 5:15 link.

   c. At the top of the page, click Dewey.

   d. On the next page, click 300 Social sciences.

   e. On the next page, click 310 Collections of general statistics.

   f. On the next page, click 317.3 Statistics of the United States and Canada.

   g. In the Skill #4 table in the Data File record the total number of Web sites listed under this link.

   h. Look through the links and their annotations. Choose one that you think might be useful for your brother. In the Skill #4 table in the Data File, record its title and URL, then save the Data File.

5. Tap a trailblazer page.

   a. You are still keeping your eye open for online career material for your friend and have just run across The Occupational Outlook Handbook. You want to decide quickly if this is one that you want to share with her.

   b. Go to the Student Online Companion and click the Occupational Outlook Handbook link under "Specialized search engines."

   c. Answer the questions posed in the Skill #5 table in the Data File, then save the Data File.

6. **Use a specialized search engine.**

   a. You remember reading this great quote from Wayne Gretzky but can't quite recall how it was worded. It had something to do with **100% of your shots**. You decide to try a specialty subject engine to find it.

   b. Go to the Student Online Companion and click the Quoteland.com link (under Specialized search engines).

   c. Type **Gretzky** in the search form, then click Search.

   d. Follow the link that Quoteland returns for **Wayne Gretzky**.

   e. Look at the quotes on the results page, identify the one you are looking for, record the quote in the Skill #6 table in the Data File, then save the Data File.

7. **Understand evaluative criteria.**

   a. In the Skill #7 box in the Data File, identify at least three criteria for evaluating Web pages for appropriateness.

   b. In the Skill #7 box in the Data File, write a few sentences about each of the three criteria, including why the criteria is important and sample questions to answer to determine if the page meets the criteria.

   c. Save the Data File.

8. **Evaluate a Web page.**

   a. You are writing a paper on the history of mathematics. You found a Web page that might be relevant and want to evaluate it quickly.

   b. Go to the Student Online Companion, and click the MacTutor History of Mathematics link (under Specialized search engines).

   c. Answer the questions in the Skill #8 table in the Data File, then save and close the Data File.

▼ INDEPENDENT CHALLENGE 1

Your company is thinking of designing new billboards and the graphic artist, who wants to use a retro look in one of her proposals, asks if you could help her find examples of World War II poster art. You want to find something for her that you're sure is of good quality, so you turn to the INFOMINE subject guide.

   a. Open the Student Online Companion at **www.course.com/illustrated/research2**, and click INFOMINE.

   b. There are a couple of potential broad headings on the home page that might produce good results. You decide to click **Government Info** first.

   c. When the search page opens, scroll down to **Browse Options**, and under **Subjects** click **LCSH** (for Library of Congress Subject Headings).

   d. You see a list of the alphabet so decide to go for a possible World War II heading and click W.

   e. There are so many *W*s that you now must click **We – Wr**.

   f. Scroll down the alphabetical list until you find **World War, 1939 – 1945 – Posters**, and click the heading.

   g. Open a file in your word processor and record the titles of the sites indexed.

   h. Add your name to the document and save it as **Unit C IC1.doc**.

Advanced Challenge Exercise

   ■ Click the link for World War II Poster Database.

   ■ Look over the site and identify ways to use it.

   ■ In the same text file, write about how one can search this site.

   ■ Perform a search and identify a poster you find interesting, then click Display the full record to find out more about it.

   ■ In the text file, describe your search and provide information about the poster you selected.

   i. Save, print, and close the file.

Internet Research

▼ INDEPENDENT CHALLENGE 2

You are beginning a new job working with a team of Web developers. You'd like to find some highly recommended sites that you can bookmark for future use. You are interested in sites about creating Web pages using the Web coding language HTML.

    a. In your word processor open a new file, add your name to the file, save it as **Unit C IC2.doc**, then go to lii.org.

    b. Find their recommended Web sites for HTML.

    c. In your text file, record how many Web sites lii.org lists under the topic **HTML–Document markup language**. (*Hint*: The number listed under this topic is fewer than the number of sites that have HTML anywhere in the title or annotation.)

    d. How did you find these sites? In your file, list the steps you took to find them, then save, print, and close the file.

▼ INDEPENDENT CHALLENGE 3

The health care provider you work for has just made a new Web page. The managers found the Web site shown in Figure C-22 and would like you to evaluate it for them. Is it credible and good enough to include as a link on their Web page? They would like you to present a list of reasons why it should or should not be included.

    a. Open your browser and find this page on the Web.

    b. Evaluate the Web site by answering questions about its organization, authority, scope, objectivity, and currency.

    c. In your word processor, open a new document, save it as **Unit C IC3.doc**, then document your thoughts on why this site would or would not be an appropriate Web site to link to your employer's site.

    d. Include at least five reasons in your argument.

    e. Add your name to the document, then save, print, and close it.

FIGURE C-22

INDEPENDENT CHALLENGE 4

You have a class assignment due for which you must use a credible Web site as one of your sources for a paper covering a topic of your choosing. You want to use a subject guide of academic quality to locate an appropriate site.

   a. Go to a subject guide.

   b. Find a few sources that you think might be useful.

   c. In your word processor, open a new document, save it as **Unit C IC4.doc,** then describe which subject guide you used and how you searched (local search engine, drilling down, or another method).

   d. How many sites did you find related to your topic?

   e. Select one site that you think might be particularly relevant and evaluate it according to these criteria: organization, authority, scope, objectivity, and currency. Write at least one sentence about how the site meets each criterion.

   f. Would you say this is an appropriate and credible Web site for your assignment?

   g. Add your name to the document, then save it.

Advanced Challenge Exercise

- You want to do another search to check for a site you might like better than the one you found in your last search, so you select a different subject guide.
- Find relevant sites.
- In the same text file, describe how you searched (search or drilling down) and record how many sites you found.
- Write a sentence about which subject guide was the most user friendly and which provided the single best result.

   h. Save, print, and close the text file, then exit your word-processing program.

▼ VISUAL WORKSHOP

During your exploration of subject guides you found and printed this page. Find this subject guide online and quickly evaluate it. Print the page, note at the top of the page if you think it *is* or *is not* appropriate for you to use in the future as a hockey resource, then write your name at the top.

FIGURE C-23

hockeyDB.com

The Internet Hockey Database

Welcome to hockeydb.com, the internet's largest repository of hockey data!

Stop Stealing Content with Site Suckers

Quick Surf

📁 **Statistics**
├📁 **Player Search**
├📁 **Standings & Rosters**
├📁 **Team Records**
├📁 **Current Team Guides**
├📁 **Current Scoring**
├📁 **All-Time Records**
📁 **Draft Picks**
├📁 **by Year**
├📁 **by Team**
📁 **Logos**
├📁 **by League**
├📁 **by Team**

Statistics Archive

The standings and player statistics for nearly every professional hockey player to play -- ever! You will find information for almost all professional leagues that iced a team -- not just the NHL. And there is a tremendous amount of amateur stats listed as well.

Draft Pick Archive

Here is an archive of all the amateur players ever drafted in both the NHL and WHA drafts. You can view each draft class to see their NHL/WHA performance, and you can look up all the draft picks by your favorite team.

Logo Archive

There have been hundreds of teams to play professional hockey over the years. Every year a dozen more seem to pop up. You can now see the logos of many of those teams in this archive.

Trading Card Archive

This archive contains checklists of nearly every hockey card set ever made. There is a wealth of information on minor league card sets. In addition you can get a checklist of nearly any hockey player, both NHL and minor pro, who has a trading card.

NHL Player Lists

This archive features different ways of looking at NHL players. You can see an alphabetical list of every NHL player, a list of players who only played in a single NHL game, or a list of players who only appeared in the NHL playoffs.

Player Awards

Auctions by Hockeydb

Attention Journalists! New Feature!

Use Hockeydb.com's **Player Encoder** to enhance your hockey articles. The encoder creates links to hockeydb.com's player statistics for every player mentioned in the article. Give it a try!

Administration

◉ **Feedback**
◉ **FAQ**
◉ **Credits**
◉ **Advertising**
◉ **Links**

Finding Specialty Information

OBJECTIVES

Understand specialty information
Find people and places
Locate businesses
Search periodical databases
Find government information
Find online reference sources
Find mailing lists and newsgroups
Search with intelligent agents

You have already learned to use search engines and subject guides for general research. However, sometimes the information you want is very specific, such as someone's name, the address of a business, or the definition of a word. This kind of specialty information is often stored in online databases that require direct access, making traditional search engines and most subject guides ineffective. Specialty information is accessed through specialty Web sites that include online telephone directories, maps, periodicals, government sites, mailing lists, and newsgroups. Until recently, you had to visit each of these specialty Web sites to retrieve information. Fortunately, a new breed of software called "intelligent search agents" can automate this process by simultaneously retrieving information stored in many of these Web databases. ▨▨▨ You will be attending a conference in Washington, D.C. on renewable energy. In preparing for this conference, Jane suggests you continue your research on alternative energy using specialty Web sites and intelligent search agents.

Understanding Specialty Information

By far, the largest part of the Internet is hidden from most search tools. This hidden content is called the **deep Web** or the **invisible Web**. The search engines you have used so far have searched for information on the **visible Web**, which is the portion of the Web indexed by search engine spiders. Deep Web content largely resides in online databases and is unavailable to traditional search engines and subject guides because they require direct queries at their sites. Common examples of online databases are online phone books or newspaper and magazine archives. Other examples include **dynamically generated Web pages** that a database creates based on a specific query, or pages that require a login name and password. Pages that are not in HTML format, such as .pdf or .doc files, can also be hard for search engine spiders to index. Figure D-1 provides a conceptual view of the differences between the invisible and the visible Web and the areas searched by search engines and subject guides versus the areas searched by intelligent search agents and specialty search tools. Not wanting to ignore a large part of the information available via the Internet, you decide to learn about research tools that can help make the invisible Web usable. Jane provides some basics on using these specialty search tools.

DETAILS

Some important points to remember are:

- **How to find specialty information**
  Typically, you locate invisible Web content by going to a specialty Web site and using its search form to query a database. Although the vast majority of the invisible Web is available publicly, some specialized databases require subscriptions. Because libraries pay the subscription fees for many of these specialty sites, such as the full-text magazine and newspaper article databases ProQuest, EBSCOhost, and InfoTrac, they are a good place to access these resources. You can also go to a "virtual library" such as the Internet Public Library (www.ipl.org), which links to these specialty Web sites from its reference section.

QUICK TIP

Be sure to read the About information at a specialty site before using it.

- **Scope and focus**
  By definition, specialty Web sites tend to have a narrower and deeper focus, usually resulting in higher-quality content. However, even two tools that focus on the same narrow area are not exactly alike. For example, various governmental agencies are charged with creating access to different, but sometimes overlapping, government information. The National Technical Information Service (NTIS) has a database of publications on scientific, technical, and business-related topics. The U.S. Census Bureau Web site primarily focuses on Web sites containing demographic information, but also features data related to business, as well as Census Bureau products, such as CD-ROMs and DVDs for sale. The Government Printing Office (GPO) is charged with making much of the information produced by the federal government accessible to citizens. State governments also usually provide their own searchable sites.

QUICK TIP

After registering with some "free" sites, you may see an increase in promotional e-mail, either from the site itself or from businesses to which they sold your address. This is the true price you pay for giving the site personal information. Always review the site's privacy information before sharing your address.

- **Free or pay?**
  Most specialty Web sites are either free or partially free. If they are commercial sites, they may give away some information but charge you for detailed data. Other sites might allow you free access, but require you to register with them—some require only an e-mail address or user name and others require considerably more personal information. Some sites, including many newspaper sites, allow free access to their most recent files, but charge for access to archival files. If a site is going to charge you up front, it asks you for your credit card number—so don't give it out unless you want them to use it.

- **Incomplete coverage**
  Up-to-date, detailed information about people or businesses is hard to come by and therefore valuable. Companies guard proprietary information with security measures that prevent unauthorized access. So, although specialty Web sites provide access to much of the invisible Web, portions remain hidden.

- **Automatic searches**
  A new breed of software called an **intelligent search agent** now makes it possible to automatically retrieve information stored in multiple databases on the Web. An intelligent search agent can simultaneously query hundreds of databases (the invisible Web) as well as traditional online resources (the visible Web). An intelligent search agent "knows" how to query each online database, thus eliminating the need to visit individual sites and manually enter queries. However, you still need to manually search specialty databases that require fees or passwords.

FIGURE D-1: The visible and invisible Web

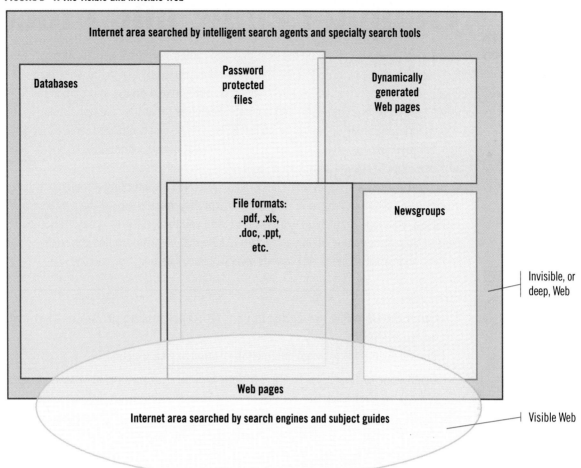

Internet area searched by intelligent search agents and specialty search tools

Databases

Password protected files

Dynamically generated Web pages

File formats: .pdf, .xls, .doc, .ppt, etc.

Newsgroups

Invisible, or deep, Web

Web pages

Internet area searched by search engines and subject guides

Visible Web

Clues to Use

Visible and invisible Web

According to a white paper from Bright Planet (makers of DQM, an intelligent search agent), the invisible or deep Web is 500 times larger than the visible or surface Web (to see this white paper, click the Deep Web link under "Invisible Web" in the Student Online Companion). The visible or surface Web accounts for only about 13 billion pages, while the deep Web contains approximately five trillion pages hidden from the view of traditional search engines. Approximately 95% of the invisible Web is available publicly (i.e., it doesn't require a fee or password). For more information about the invisible Web, click the links under "Invisible Web" in the Student Online Companion.

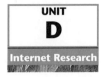
Finding People and Places

There are a variety of services on the Web that allow you to search for people. At most of them, you can search for a person's phone number and street address just as you would search the white pages of a local phone book. Phone number and street address information is usually based on the information found in telephone books, which tend to be both thorough and accurate. Remember that they are not absolutely comprehensive, however, as individuals may opt out of being listed. There is no real centralized service that gathers e-mail information. Some white pages sites allow searching for e-mail addresses, although you should keep in mind that e-mail addresses tend to change fairly frequently, making this kind of search less successful. ▰▰▰▰ The Department of Energy Efficiency and Renewable Energy Network (EERE) is sponsoring a conference in Washington, D.C., for government officials interested in renewable energy. You plan to attend the conference. While you're on the East coast, you hope to catch up with a relative who you think still lives in New York City. This relative just happens to share your name. When you explain to Jane that you want to find the relative's phone number, street address, and e-mail address, she suggests several online directories you can try.

STEPS

1. **Open the Data File IR-UD.doc in your word-processing program, then save it as Specialty Information.doc**

   You will use this file to record information you find in your searches.

   QUICK TIP
   You do not need to use capital letters when searching names of people, cities, businesses, and so on.

2. **Open your browser, go to the Student Online Companion at www.course.com/illustrated/research2, then click the Yahoo! People Search link (under "White Pages")**

   The Yahoo! People Search home page appears. You enter your information in the text boxes provided as shown in Figure D-2. Notice that directory searches often provide better results using just an initial, rather than a first name.

   TROUBLE
   If there are no results, try your search again and leave the First Name text box empty or enter another name.

3. **Type your first initial in the First Name text box, your last name in the Last Name text box, New York in the City/Town text box, NY in the State text box, then click the Search button**

   A list of names should appear, as shown in Figure D-3. Notice on the right side of the page are links for an Advanced Search using USSearch.com. This kind of search requires you to pay a fee, which is often substantial, by using your credit card online.

4. **Choose one name and phone number, then record it in the Lesson 2 table in the Data File**

5. **Click the name (it should be underlined on your screen)**

   A separate page appears with your person's personal data. You decide to see if you can find an e-mail address.

6. **Go to the Student Online Companion, click the White Pages—DogPile link (under "White Pages"), then click the Email Search link**

   DogPile's Email search page appears.

   TROUBLE
   If there are no results, try your search again and leave the First Name text box empty or enter another name.

7. **Type your first initial in the First Name text box, type your last name in the Last Name text box, type New York in the City text box, select New York from the State list box, then click the Find button**

   A list of names should appear, as shown in Figure D-4. Notice that near the bottom of the page you have the option of using DogPile to search Canada, the U.K. or other international directories.

   QUICK TIP
   There are other e-mail directory services listed in the Student Online Companion.

8. **Scroll through the results list, select a name, use the Lesson 2 table in the Data File to enter the name and the information provided for an e-mail address of the person, then save the Data File**

   The name you select may have a little or a lot of information, depending on how much information the person provided.

FIGURE D-2: Yahoo! People Search

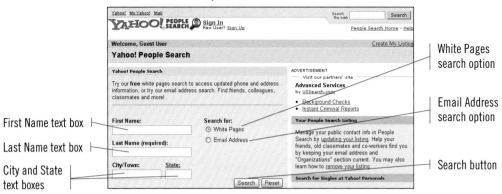

First Name text box ⊢

Last Name text box ⊢

City and State
text boxes ⊢

White Pages
search option

Email Address
search option

Search button

FIGURE D-3: Yahoo! People Search results

Your search ⊢

Search results ⊢

Create My Listing link

Advanced Services link

Update and remove your
listing links

FIGURE D-4: DogPile Email Search results

Your search ⊢

How DogPile
interpreted your
search

Search results ⊢

Notice that DogPile
inserted the AND
symbol in your
search

Number of results

Clues to Use

Finding places

Before the World Wide Web, you had to buy a map or go to the library to find out how to get where you wanted to go. Now the Web offers quite a few good map and locator Web sites. Many of these sites also provide trip planners and driving directions. In addition, they provide links to hotels, historical sites, and other attractions along the way. The Student Online Companion provides links to map sites with driving directions for the United States, such as Maps On Us and Yahoo! Maps. Yahoo! Maps also covers Canada, the UK, Spain, Italy, Germany, and France. MapQuest has sites specific to many countries as well, including the United Kingdom (www.mapquest.co.uk), Germany (www.mapquest.de), and France (www.mapquest.fr).

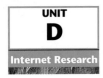

Locating Businesses

Just as there are many sites for finding people and places on the Web, there are also many yellow pages sites for finding businesses in the United States and worldwide, as shown in Table D-1. The site AnyWho (listed in the Student Online Companion) provides a list of international directories. The most high-powered business finders, such as Switchboard.com, integrate business directory listings with maps and travel planners. Most of the yellow pages directories on the Web build their databases from accurate and up-to-date information and allow new businesses to add their own information at any time. There is no charge to a business for the basic address and telephone listings. However, if a business wants to include a link to its Web site or an advertisement, it is charged for the service. ██████ While you are in Washington, D.C., you plan to meet with an expert in wind energy legislation. You need directions to her office. You remember that the name of the organization is something like "Wind Energy," and it's either in Washington, D.C., or Arlington, Virginia. Jane suggests using Switchboard.com.

STEPS

QUICK TIP
In a directory data-base such as Switch-board, *not* entering all your data at once can sometimes be a good search strategy.

1. **Go to the Student Online Companion at** www.course.com/illustrated/research2, **then click the** Switchboard link **(under "Yellow Pages")**
The Switchboard Web site appears. You can use this Web site to find a person, a business, or a product.

2. **Make sure the Find a Business option button is selected, then click the** Advanced search link
The Switchboard Find a Business advanced search form appears.

3. **Click the** Search Near a Location option button, **if necessary, click the** And / Or Search by Business Name text box **and type** wind energy, **click the** City text box **and type** arlington, **click the** State text box **and type** va, **then click the** SEARCH button
Your Find a Business advanced search form should look similar to Figure D-5. Figure D-6 illustrates your results. You see that the office for which you were looking, American Wind Energy, is listed as being on C Street NW in Washington, D.C. Now you'd like to see a map.

4. **Click the** Map link **under the listing for American Wind Energy**
You note the location, and because you'll be in the area at lunchtime, you decide to see what restaurants are nearby.

5. **Click your browser's** Back button **to return to the listing, click the** What's Nearby? link, **scroll if necessary, click the** Restaurants link **under Food and Dining, then click the** Restaurants-Pizza link
The search results appear as shown in Figure D-7.

6. **Choose a pizzeria from the list that appears, record the name and address in the Lesson 3 table in the Data File, then save the Data File**

TABLE D-1: Features of business finder Web sites (see the Student Online Companion)

name	country	people	business	toll-free numbers	maps	city pages
AnyWho	USA	X	X	X	X	
Canada411	Canada	X	X			
Europages	Europe		X			
Scoot	UK, France, Belgium, Netherlands		X			
SuperPages	USA	X	X		X	X
Switchboard	USA	X	X		X	X
UKphonebook	UK	X	X			
Yell.com	UK		X			
Yellowpages.ca	Canada	X	X	X		X
Yellowpages.com.au	Australia	X	X		X	

FIGURE D-5: Switchboard's Find a Business advanced search form

Find a Business advanced search form

Option to search in or near a location

Categories/Keyword(s) text box

And/Or Search by Business Name text box

City and State text boxes

Option to search by business category

Option to specify how far from a location you wish to search

Log of your recent searches

Zip code text box

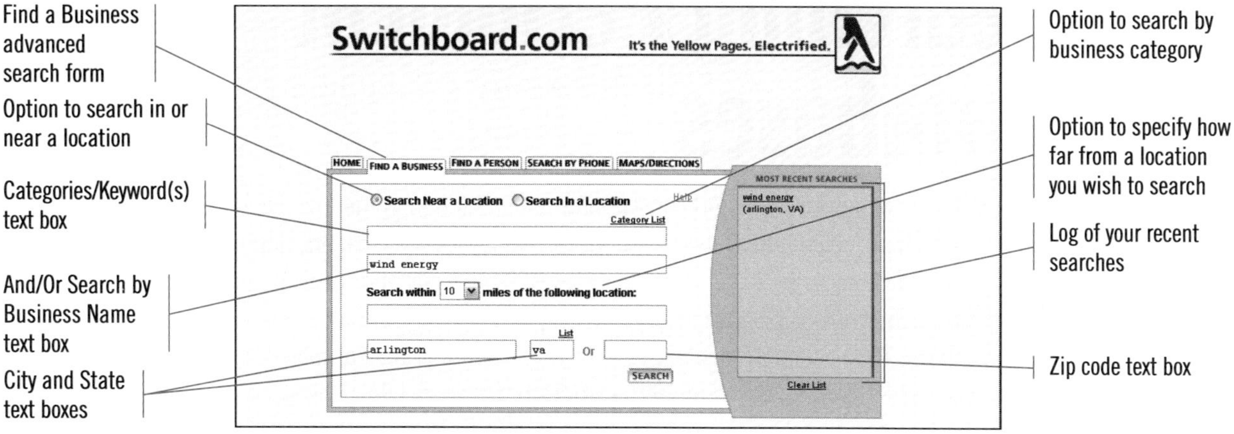

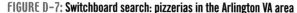

FIGURE D-6: Switchboard search: *wind energy* near *Arlington, VA*

Your search results

Options for further information

Option to modify your search

Your search

Sponsored results

FIGURE D-7: Switchboard search: pizzerias in the Arlington VA area

Your search results

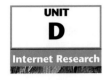
Searching Periodical Databases

Some of the most authoritative and current information hidden in the invisible Web is stored in **periodical databases**. These include the archives of popular magazines, newspapers, and scholarly journals. Table D-2 describes the differences between different types of periodicals and gives an example of each type. Some periodicals, such as *Salon* or *First Monday*, exist only in electronic format on the Web. Other periodicals, such as *The Times* or *The New York Times*, have an online version that may or may not carry all the same stories as the printed version, and may include some stories not seen in print. There are also subscription databases such as ProQuest and InfoTrac, available at libraries, which store electronic versions of thousands of periodical titles. Most online periodical databases give out limited recent information for free, but require registration or payment for older materials. Before leaving for the conference in Washington, D.C., you decide to look for some current articles on alternative energy topics that you can read on the plane. Jane provides a list of potential databases and you decide to begin with *The Times* from London.

STEPS

1. **Go to the Student Online Companion at** www.course.com/illustrated/research2, **then click The Times link (under "Periodical listings")**

   The TimesOnline home page appears.

   TROUBLE
   If your search did not find any articles, try another search using another alternative energy topic. If your search still does not yield any articles, enter any other keywords.

2. **Type** "renewable energy" **in the** Search text box, **then click the** GO button

   The Times Search Panel opens in a new window, giving you the option to Search the Times Web site or to search the Web.

3. **Click the** Search button **in the Search the Site box**

   A new TimesOnline window opens listing your search results with links to relevant articles, as shown in Figure D-8. As you study the page, note the message under "SEARCHTIPS" stating that articles published within the last seven days are free, but there is a charge for older articles. A percentage figure appears beside each article indicating the article's relevance to your search. You want to read an article.

   TROUBLE
   If a login box opens for the article you choose, close it and click the title of a different article.

4. **Click the** title **of an article, open it, then record the article title in the Lesson 4 table in the Data File**

   Next, you want to try searching a larger periodical database.

5. **Go to the** Student Online Companion, **then click the** MagPortal.com link **(under "Periodical listings")**

   The MagPortal site appears. Notice the site offers broad topical categories you can navigate by drilling down to find articles of interest. The site also offers a Search text box to use for searching on keywords.

6. **Type** "renewable energy" **in the Search text box, then click the** Search button

   A list of online articles with brief annotations appears, as shown in Figure D-9. The small wavy line icon at the end of each article links you to similar articles.

7. **Click the** title **of one of the articles**

   You should be taken from the MagPortal Web site to the publication site.

8. **Record the article title in the Lesson 4 table in the Data File, then save the Data File**

FIGURE D-8: TimesOnline search: "renewable energy"

Number of results

Your search results

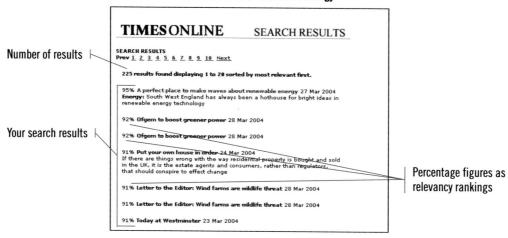

Percentage figures as relevancy rankings

FIGURE D-9: MagPortal search: "renewable energy"

Number of results

Your search results

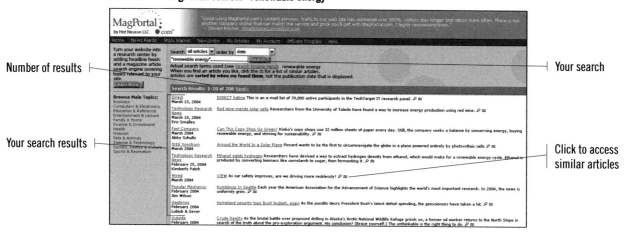

Your search

Click to access similar articles

TABLE D-2: Periodicals and their distinguishing characteristics

periodical type	purpose	publisher	audience	documentation	example
Scholarly/research	Original research/ experiments	University/ organization	Scholars/ professionals/ university students	Citations/ bibliography	*Harvard Education Review*
Professional/ special interest	Professional practice/ case studies	Organization	Professionals/ university students	May cite or provide bibliography	*Journal of Accountancy*
General interest	Inform/entertain/ advocate	Commercial	Knowledgeable reader/possibly technical	May mention sources	*The New York Times*
popular	Entertain	Commercial	General audience/ simple language	Rarely mentions sources	*Metropolitan Home*

Clues to Use

Where to find online periodicals

There are some sites on the Web that are "online newsstands." They collect links to electronic periodicals from around the world on all topics. Examples are provided in the Student Online Companion. They include the Internet Public Library Online Serials collection, the Librarians' Index to the Internet Magazine Topics, and NewsDirectory.com. Other sites such as MagPortal.com and FindArticles allow you to search many online magazine databases simultaneously. The most comprehensive online databases, such as ProQuest and InfoTrac, are available through public, school, and academic libraries. As long as you are affiliated with a library you can access these databases from home at no charge—just ask your local librarian how.

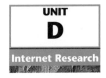

Finding Government Information

Governments are prodigious producers and users of information. Large gateways, called **portals**, create access to different segments of government information, as shown in Table D-3. Portals originated in the commercial sector with sites such as America Online and MSN that offered "everything"—search engines, news, shopping, e-mail, chat, and more. They each endeavored to create such an attractive and useful site that you would never go anywhere else to find information. The idea of a portal caught on and now many other sites have carved out niches in various subject areas, especially in industry and government. These portals, which are limited by subject, are also referred to as **vortals**, or vertical portals. Government portals can give you access to online information or to printed materials that you can purchase from government agencies or borrow from libraries. While attending the EERE conference in Washington, D.C., you heard of a good place to access government information online—FirstGov. You also want to see if you can find information about a project you heard discussed by attendees at the conference, called "Million solar roofs."

STEPS

QUICK TIP

Make sure the Data File is still open in your word processor.

1. **Go to the Student Online Companion at** www.course.com/illustrated/research2, **then click the** FirstGov **link (under "Government references")**

   The FirstGov Web site appears. You use the topic of "solar energy" as a test case.

2. **Type** "solar energy" **in the Search text box, then click the** Go button

   A list of search results appears, as shown in Figure D-10. Note that FirstGov defaults to searching for federal information, but you can change this by clicking the State or Both option buttons.

3. **Scroll through the results, select one site and record its URL in the Lesson 5 table in the Data File**

   Now you'd like to find information on "Million solar roofs."

4. **Click the** Advanced Search link

   The FirstGov Advanced Search form appears.

5. **Type** million solar roofs **in the Find these key words text box, click the** Search for list arrow, **and click** The exact phrase, **then click the** Search button

   Your search results appear. Now you want to limit this search so that all the results also include Portland and Oregon.

6. **Click the** Revise Search button

   The Advanced Search form reappears.

7. **Under the Include or exclude these words from results section of the form, in the first text box, type** portland oregon, **as shown in Figure D-11, then click the** Search button

   Your search results appear.

8. **Select one site from your results, record the URL in the Lesson 5 table in the Data File, then save the Data File**

FIGURE D-10: FirstGov search: "solar energy"

Search form

Search defaults to
Federal information

Your results

Advanced Search
options

Search tips

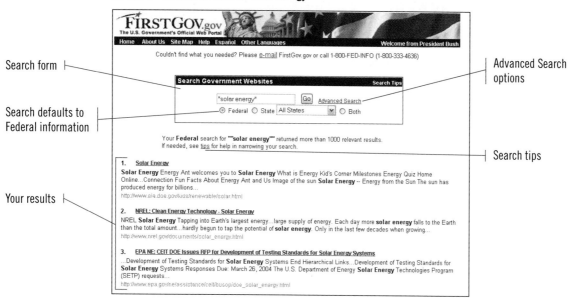

FIGURE D-11: FirstGov results: "million solar roofs" "portland oregon"

Your initial search
phrase

Your search refined
with the additional
keywords

Ways to refine your
search, including by
format, language,
AND, OR, AND NOT,
domain, sorting
options, and more

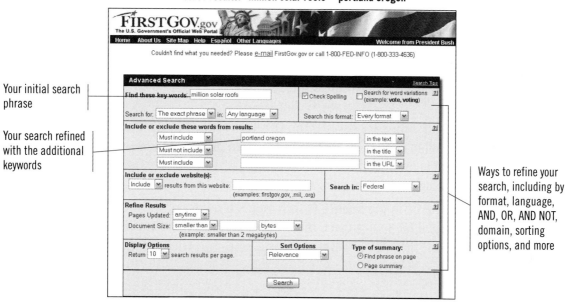

TABLE D-3: Specialized government portals (see the Student Online Companion)

name	features
Australian Commonwealth Government Information	Australian federal and state information
Canadian Government Information on the Internet	Canadian federal, provincial, and municipal information
FedWorld (US)	Sponsored by the National Technical Information Service (NTIS). Covers scientific, technical, and engineering information. Some links to government Web sites. Most links to reports and publications available for purchase.
FirstGov (US)	Most comprehensive site for U.S. government information online. Links to over 20,000 federal and state government Web sites.
DirectGov	Central and local government information for the United Kingdom
U.S. Government Printing Office	Links to federal publications. Provides catalog of government documents available for purchase. Catalog of libraries that own specific documents.
University of Michigan Documents Center	Most complete guide to government information. Links to government sites, including local, state, federal, and international.

Internet Research

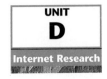
Finding Online Reference Sources

Online reference sources are similar to their counterparts on library shelves. They include almanacs, dictionaries, directories, and encyclopedias—the kinds of references you don't read cover to cover, but refer to often. Library Web sites almost always link to a variety of online reference sources, some of them licensed exclusively for their patrons' use. There are also virtual libraries, such as the Internet Public Library, that exist solely to bring together valuable Web sites and reference tools. ▇▇▇▇▇ You have returned from the EERE conference and you are ready to finish your final list of alternative energy Web resources, but would like to find a few reliable online reference resources. Jane suggests looking through the reference sources at ipl, The Internet Public Library.

STEPS

QUICK TIP

It's a good idea, once you've found a few good reference sites, to include them in your browser's Favorites or Bookmarks file for easy access.

1. **Go to the Student Online Companion at** www.course.com/illustrated/research2, **click the ipl Reference Page link (under "Online references"), then click** Subject Collections

   The Internet Public Library main subject categories page appears. You want to look over the reference sources indexed here.

2. **Click** Ready Reference, **click** Census Data & Demographics, **scroll the page to locate and then click** Statistical Resources on the Web

   This link takes you to the University of Michigan Documents Center Web page. You decide to return to the ipl site and view the Energy subject category.

3. **Click your browser's** Back button **to return to the Census Data and Demographics links at ipl, scroll back to the top of the page, then place your cursor over the** Science & Tech link **under the list of Subject Collections**

   A cascading menu appears listing subtopics.

4. **Click** Energy **in the Science & Tech menu, browse the resources, select one link that might be helpful for your project, then record the URL in the Lesson 6 table in the Data File**

   Figure D-12 shows the ipl Energy reference resources page. While scanning this page, you notice that one ipl category is KidSpace, so you decide to see if there is an alternative energy site for children that you might want to include.

5. **Click** KidSpace, **type** renewable energy **in the Search text box, click the** Search button, **and then click the link to** View all results

   Figure D-13 illustrates your results.

6. **Select a page to include in your report, record the URL in the Lesson 6 table in the Data File, then save the Data File**

FIGURE D-12: ipl energy reference sources

Path showing where you are as you drill down into subject categories

Subject categories which open menus to subtopics

Search form

Annotated resource links

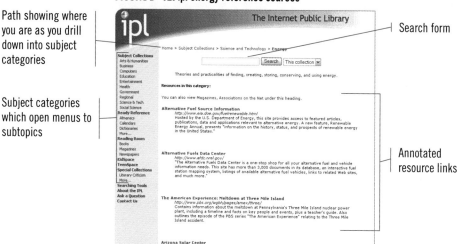

FIGURE D-13: ipl KidSpace search: *renewable energy*

Number of results for sites appropriate for children

Annotated resource links

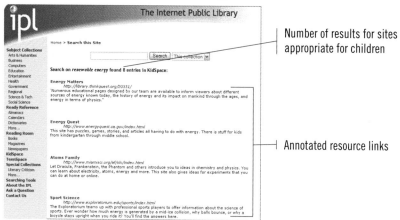

Clues to Use

Online reference sources about the Internet

The Web includes reference sources on just about any topic. If you are working on a special research topic, you can always find good sources at the Reference sections of the Internet Public Library or the Librarians' Index to the Internet and add them temporarily to your browser's Bookmark or Favorite files. For instance, if you were studying the Internet, the following might be good sources to have close at hand:

name	resource type	features
FILExt	Dictionary	Lists most Internet file extensions. Defines extensions and links to more information.
Netiquette Home Page	Book	Provides the basics of Netiquette, at work and at home. Covers primarily e-mail and newsgroups.
Webopedia	Dictionary/encyclopedia	Covers computer and Internet terminology. Provides paragraph definitions and links.
Living Internet	Encyclopedia	Covers the Internet, the Web, e-mail, chat, newsgroups, and mailing lists. Articles include history and how-to information.
Internet Tutorials (Univ. of Albany Libraries)	Tutorial	Covers Using the Web, Searching the Web, Browsers, and Training. Provides links and how-to tips.
lii.org (Internet Topics Page)	Subject guide	Provides reliable links to answer almost any Internet question. Covers searching, Web design, history, law, children, and more.

Finding Mailing Lists and Newsgroups

The Internet is more than just its Web documents; it also provides a variety of ways to communicate and interact with other people. On the Web, you can instantly become part of discussions of current issues and breaking news by subscribing to a **mailing list**, which allows you to e-mail messages to all other members of the list automatically. Mailing lists are often called **listservs** after the software that supports them. Another major method of information exchange on the Internet is **newsgroups**, virtual bulletin boards where messages on thousands of topics are posted daily. Newsgroups are often referred to as **Usenet** after the system that distributes them. Anyone on the Internet can read and respond to the postings in a newsgroup, though you may be required to register. As the posted topics diverge, they are broken off into different **threads**, or subtopics. By searching the archives of discussion postings, you can also tap into primary documents that follow the development of topics from many personal and unconventional angles. You can find links to mailing lists and newsgroups about specific subjects on trailblazer Web pages, or you can search specific sites that list mailing lists or newsgroups. 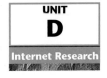 The EERE conference in Washington, D.C., was a great opportunity to meet people interested in alternative energy sources. Jane suggests you continue to communicate with other people who are interested in alternative energy topics through discussion groups. You remember seeing energy related discussion groups when searching EERE's site, so decide to start there.

STEPS

1. **Go to the Student Online Companion at** www.course.com/illustrated/research2, **click the** EERE link **(under "Subject guides"), click the** Bioenergy link **under Renewable Energy, then click the** Discussion Groups link **under Bioenergy Organizations & Resources**

    A page of links to newsgroups and mailing lists appears, as shown in Figure D-14.

QUICK TIP

Subscription addresses are in the following format: *listname-subscribe@ someplace.org.*

2. **Click a** mailing list **that seems interesting, find the** subscription address **at its Web site, use the Lesson 7 table in the Data File to record the address, then save and close the Data File and close your word-processing program**

QUICK TIP

Newsgroup names are hierarchical and mnemonic. For example, a recreational group that discusses horses might be called *rec.equestrian.* Different parts of the name are separated by periods.

3. **Go to the** Student Online Companion, **click the** Google link **(under "Search engines"), then click the** Groups link

    Note that there is a Search text box where you can search the archives of Usenet postings with keywords. You decide that your topic, alternative energy, is probably listed under **sci**.

4. **Click the word** sci.

    Groups that have the prefix **sci** are the science-related newsgroups. The bars to the left of the names of the newsgroups indicate the relative volume of messages posted.

5. **Scroll down the page and click the** sci.energy link

    A list of postings to the sci.energy newsgroup appears, as shown in Figure D-15. This is the archive of the various newsgroup threads.

QUICK TIP

To participate in a sci.energy thread, click it, then click Post a new message. However, you will need to register first.

6. **Scroll down the page and find a thread of interest to you, then print one page of the postings and write your name at the top of the page**

    You are interested in reading more about the uses and development of Usenet Newsgroups.

7. **Go to the** Student Online Companion, **click the** Development of Usenet link **(under "Online references"), then read the article entitled "The Social Forces Behind the Development of Usenet"**

FIGURE D-14: Bioenergy discussion groups

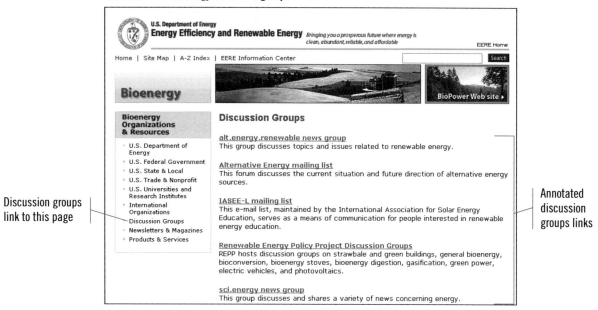

Discussion groups link to this page

Annotated discussion groups links

FIGURE D-15: Google newsgroup sci.energy

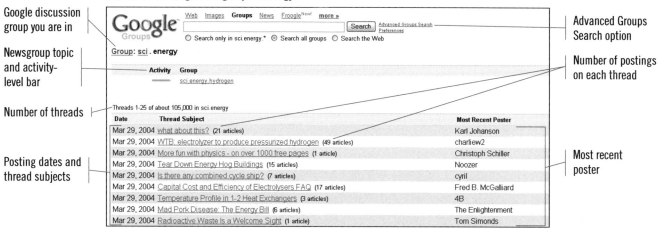

Google discussion group you are in

Newsgroup topic and activity-level bar

Number of threads

Posting dates and thread subjects

Advanced Groups Search option

Number of postings on each thread

Most recent poster

Clues to Use

Netiquette

Netiquette is the protocol and common rules of courtesy used by people on the Internet. For example, when you use a mailing list, you need to know that there are two separate e-mail addresses that have very different functions. You use the subscription address (also known as the administrative address) to send messages asking the administrator to add or drop your name from the list. The list address is the place to send your actual list correspondence. If you use the wrong address and send your subscription information to the 10,000 or more members of a list, more than one may e-mail you and politely let you know that you should use the *other* address.

(If any member e-mails you and *impolitely* tells you to use the other address, this is called a "flame.")

Before you post to a newsgroup, it is good form to read the FAQ (frequently asked questions) and some of the more recent postings. In this way you will ensure that you don't post a message to an inappropriate group, or ask a question that has been answered in a recent thread. For more information on netiquette, click the Netiquette Home Page link under "Online references" in the Student Online Companion.

Internet Research

Searching with Intelligent Agents

As the Internet grows and becomes more diverse, finding the correct information is more of a challenge. Fortunately, new tools are evolving that make searching the visible and invisible parts of the Web simpler and more comprehensive. An **intelligent search agent**, or **search bot**, is a software program that automates search activities that traditional search services aren't programmed to perform, such as searching through online databases. One of the most powerful of the freely available intelligent search agents is ProFusion, which can simultaneously query multiple databases, search engines, and subject guides. ProFusion "knows" how to query each database, eliminating the need to visit individual sites and manually enter queries. In addition, ProFusion can rank and sort search results from multiple sources, making it faster and easier to find the information you need. You want to explore how an intelligent agent can make your searching more efficient and effective. Jane suggests trying ProFusion to locate the latest business information about alternative energy.

STEPS

QUICK TIP
Click the Web Search Engines link to alter the list of engines searched by ProFusion.

1. **Go to the** Student Online Companion, **and then click the** ProFusion link **(under "Intelligent search agents")**

   The ProFusion Web site appears. The Search text box at the top of the page automatically queries multiple search engines simultaneously. A list of "vertical" Search Groups appears below the Search text box. These groups enable you to target your search, using databases, specialty directories, magazine archives, and other resources. Because you are looking for business information about alternative energy, you decide to use the Business Vertical Search Group.

QUICK TIP
Click the Include Web Search Engines check box to have ProFusion perform a metasearch.

2. **Click the** Business link **in the list of vertical search groups**

   The Business page appears, displaying a list of Business search "subgroups," as shown in Figure D-16. A set of Search Options lets you control the type of search. For example, from the Search Type list box you can select All keywords, Any keywords, Boolean, or Phrase. There are also options for specifying the number of results displayed, number of results per source, and how long ProFusion waits for responses. Each Business group contains a collection of related resources.

3. **Under Search Options, click the** Search Type list box, **then click** Boolean

   The Search Type list box displays the Boolean option.

QUICK TIP
Click the Search within this group link beneath a group to alter which resources in the group are searched.

4. **Click the check boxes in front of several Business groups (e.g., Business Discussions, Business News, and Company Profiles)**

   Check marks appear in front of the chosen business groups, indicating that the preselected resources within these groups will be queried. You are now ready to enter your complex query and have ProFusion search the chosen resources.

5. **In the** Search for text box, **type** "alternative energy" OR "renewable energy", **then click the** go button

   A page with status indicators appears, showing the progress in completing the searches of the selected resources. When the searches finish, the first 10 search results appear, as shown in Figure D-17. Table D-4 lists and describes the options available on this page. The top of the page displays the total number of search results for the query. The list of results is color-coded for easy identification of key phrases in the search results. Each search result typically includes a page title, summary, and URL.

6. **Explore the most interesting search result by clicking the page title, then use the** Back button **in your browser to return to the ProFusion search results page and click the** Print Results link

   A list of search results appears in a pintable layout.

7. **Use your browser's** Print button **to print the page, write your name at the top of the printout, then close the browser**

FIGURE D-16: ProFusion Business search page

Subject categories path

Search form

Subgroups under Business

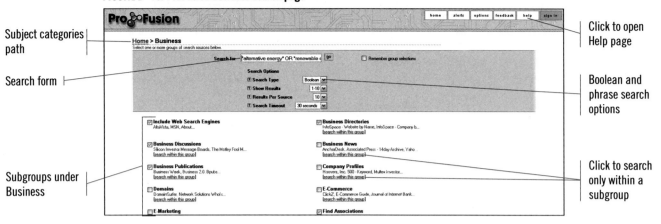

Click to open Help page

Boolean and phrase search options

Click to search only within a subgroup

FIGURE D-17: ProFusion search: "alternative energy" OR "renewable energy"

Your search

Navigation bar

Further options

Search results

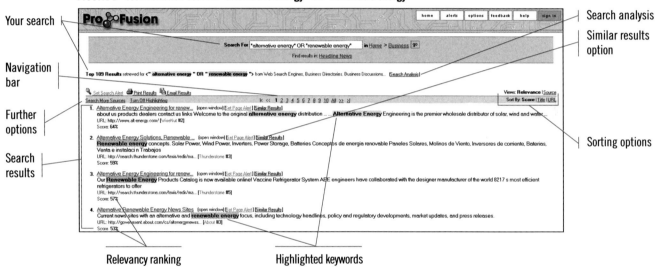

Search analysis

Similar results option

Sorting options

Relevancy ranking

Highlighted keywords

TABLE D-4: ProFusion controls for search results

control	description	control	description
Search Analysis	Provides status of each resource queried	Highlighting Off Highlighting On	Removes or displays color-coding for words and phrases
Set Search Alert	Automatically reruns the search at specified intervals	Views	Relevance—Displays results by relevance (default) Source—Displays results by search group and source
Print Results Email Results	Displays all search results formatted for printing or e-mailing (e-mailing results requires free registration)	Sort by	Score—Sorts results by relevance (default) Title—Sorts results alphabetically by title URL—Sorts results alphabetically by URL
Navigation bar	|< First page of results << Previous page of results 1...n Go to a specific page All Display all results >> Next page of results >| Last page of results	Similar Results	ProFusion analyzes the page summary, formulates a query to find similar pages, and runs it against all of the sources in the current group
Search More Sources	ProFusion queries additional related sources	Set Page Alert	Automatically sends e-mail whenever content on a specified page changes

Internet Research

Practice

▼ CONCEPTS REVIEW

Label each of the elements of the following Google Groups archive page.

FIGURE D-18

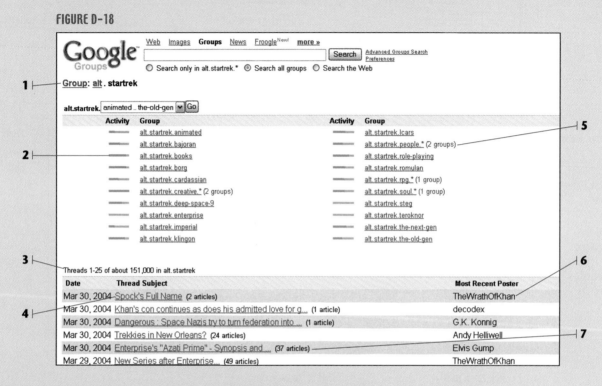

Match each term with the statement that best describes it.

8. Visible Web

9. Dynamic Web page

10. White pages

11. Yellow pages

12. Internet Public Library

13. Portal

14. Mailing list

15. Newsgroup

16. Intelligent search agent

a. Web sites with "people finder" tools

b. An example of a virtual library

c. A gateway to large segments of related Web information

d. An Internet bulletin board

e. A software program that automates search activities

f. Allows you to send and receive e-mail to and from a group of subscribers

g. The portion of the Web accessible to search engine indexing programs

h. Web sites that help you find businesses

i. A Web page that is generated when you ask for it

Select the best answer from the list of choices.

17. The invisible Web:

a. Is not accessible.

b. Consists mostly of pages written in HTML.

c. Is much smaller than the visible Web.

d. Is also known as the deep Web.

18. **You would not usually access specialty research tools by:**
    a. Asking a librarian.
    b. Using a search engine.
    c. Using a library's Web site.
    d. Using a virtual library site.

19. **Specialty sites may:**
    a. Require you to pay for the service.
    b. Allow you a few free searches and ask you to pay for more.
    c. Give away some information but charge for some too.
    d. All of the above

20. **One reason that online coverage can be incomplete is:**
    a. Companies like to give out proprietary information.
    b. Copyright law allows anyone to put current editions online.
    c. Many people value their privacy.
    d. New information has little value in today's marketplace.

21. **You would usually look for _____ at an online White pages site.**
    a. A person's address
    b. A person's e-mail address
    c. A person's phone number
    d. All of the above

22. **A good place to search for information about businesses in the UK and France is:**
    a. The Librarian's Index to the Internet.
    b. Scoot.
    c. Yellowpages.ca.
    d. Switchboard.

23. **The subtopics that appear within a newsgroup are called:**
    a. Threads.
    b. Mailing lists.
    c. Listservs.
    d. Usenets.

24. **A site that links to local, state, federal, foreign, and multinational government links is:**
    a. FirstGov.
    b. University of Michigan Documents Center.
    c. FedWorld.
    d. United States Government Printing Office.

25. **ProFusion is an example of:**
    a. A search engine.
    b. A subject guide.
    c. An intelligent search agent.
    d. A Yellow Pages site.

26. When using ProFusion, you select the resources to search by clicking:
   a. A vertical search group.
   b. A navigation arrow.
   c. The Alert Search link.
   d. None of the above

▼ SKILLS REVIEW

Reminder: You can access all of the Web sites in the Skills Review from the Student Online Companion at www.course.com/illustrated/research2.

1. Understand specialty information.

   a. Open the Data File SR-UD.doc and save it as **IR Skills Review-UD.doc**.
   b. Use the Skill #1 table in the Data File to write a sentence defining the deep or invisible Web.
   c. In the same table in the Data File, list some sources that search the deep Web.

2. Find people.

   a. Go to the Yahoo! People Search page.
   b. Type your name (or a friend's name) into the appropriate Telephone Search text boxes.
   c. Click the Search button.
   d. Click your name (or your friend's name) on the results page.
   e. Print the resulting page of information and put your name on the top.

3. Locate a business.

   a. Go to the Switchboard site and click the Find a Business option button.
   b. Type a Type of Business (or a Business Name), a City, and State, and click the Search button.
   c. Click an appropriate business category on the resulting page. (If there are no resulting businesses, go back and choose another type of business.)
   d. Scroll down the results page and find a business located in the city you chose.
   e. Click the Map link.
   f. Print the map and add your name to the top. (You may need to click the Printable Map link near the bottom of the map to get a good copy.)

4. Search periodical databases.

   a. Click the MagPortal link on the Student Online Companion.
   b. Search for a magazine article by typing your search terms in the Search text box.
   c. Scan the list of resulting articles and record one URL in the Skill # 4 table in the Data File.
   d. Click the FindArticles link at the Student Online Companion.
   e. Search for another article on the same topic.
   f. Scan the list of resulting articles at FindArticles and record one URL in the Skill #4 table in the Data File.
   g. Save and close the Data File and close your word-processing program.

5. **Find government information.**

   a. Go to the FirstGov site.

   b. Type Senator in the Search list box, choose One State, click Go, then choose a state name from the drop-down list.

   c. Click the Go button.

   d. Find a Web page with a state senator's name on it.

   e. Print the Web page and add your name to the top.

6. **Find online reference sources.**

   a. Go to the Internet Public Library Ready Reference page.

   b. Click the Style & Writing Guides link.

   c. Scroll down the page and click the Citing Electronic Resources link.

   d. Find a Web site that can help you cite documents in the APA style.

   e. Click the page name, print a copy, and add your name to the top of the page.

7. **Find a newsgroup.**

   a. Go to the Google Search engine and click the Groups link.

   b. Click a type of group of interest to you (biz., comp., sci., and so on).

   c. Choose a subgroup and click it (biz.ecommerce, comps.emacs, and so on).

   d. Find a thread of interest to you, and click that thread.

   e. Print the resulting archived message and add your name to the top.

8. **Search with an intelligent agent.**

   a. Go to ProFusion.

   b. Select a search group (e.g., Business), click one or more subgroups, and then type in a complex search query.

   c. Click the go button.

   d. Examine several of the search results.

   e. Print the first page of your search results and add your name to the top of the page.

▼ INDEPENDENT CHALLENGE 1

You and a business associate are driving from London to York to visit some clients. As you haven't driven there before, you want to get driving directions.

    a. Go to MapQuest UK.

    b. Find the section for driving directions.

    c. Enter the appropriate to and from locations and get the directions.

    d. On the resulting directions page, locate the **Redisplay Directions with** section and choose Text Only, and then click the Redisplay Directions button.

    e. Print a copy of the directions, then add your name to the top of the page.

Advanced Challenge Exercise

■ While looking for maps you decide to check the driving distance across Canada.

■ Return to MapQuest UK, click the link International Web Sites at the bottom of the page, click United States, then click the Driving Directions icon. Note the driving distance between Quebec, QC, and Vancouver, BC.

■ You realize the mileage quoted is while traveling much of the way in the United States. Because you particularly want the drive to remain in Canada, you must restate your query in several shorter trips to keep the directions within Canada. (*Hint*: You can use Quebec, QC, to Sudbury, ON, then Sudbury to Winnipeg, MB, then Winnipeg to Vancouver, BC.)

■ Print a copy of your final drive, then write the total trip mileage and your name on the top of the page.

▼ INDEPENDENT CHALLENGE 2

You are flying to Sydney, NSW, Australia, on business. You are with a firm that specializes in designing Web sites for banks. Your company is going to design the Web site for the Waratah Mortgage Corporation, and you decide to check the Web for other banks you might visit while in Sydney. You look up phone numbers and locations of banks on your laptop.

    a. Go to an appropriate Yellow Pages directory.

    b. From the information you know, set up an appropriate search.

    c. Find two banks that are located in Sydney.

    d. Print a map of each of their locations and put your name on top.

▼ INDEPENDENT CHALLENGE 3

You are thinking of immigrating to Canada and starting a business. You have heard there is a special business class immigration available.

    a. Go to an appropriate government Web site.

    b. Locate an official Canadian government Web page that has the information you need.

    c. Print the page and add your name to the top.

▼ INDEPENDENT CHALLENGE 4

You want to learn more about the content hidden in databases on the Internet. Because news articles about the invisible or deep Web are likely to be stored (or hidden) in magazine archives (databases), you decide to use the intelligent search agent ProFusion to search both the invisible (deep) Web, as well as the visible Web.

a. Go to ProFusion.

b. Scroll down the list of vertical search groups and click Technology. Click the Include Web Search Engines check box to perform a metasearch. Click several of the Technology subgroups (e.g., Tech Publications, Software Reviews, and Tech News). Click the Search Type list box and then click Boolean.

c. In the Search for text box, type "invisible Web" OR "deep Web" and then click the Go button.

d. When the search is complete, click the Title link in the Sort By: section to rearrange the search results by title.

e. Use the arrows and page numbers in the navigation bars located at the top and bottom of the page to view additional results.

f. Click several titles and find a page with useful information. Return to the ProFusion results page and click the Similar Results link to find additional pages with similar content.

g. Explore some of the new search results.

h. To share the results of this search with a friend, click the Print Results link in the ProFusion search result page. Use your browser to print a copy of the results and write your name and the title Invisible Web at the top of the printout.

i. Exit your browser.

Advanced Challenge Exercise

- You want to use a different intelligent search agent to see if it might find additional information about the invisible Web.

- Go to the Student Online Companion and click the CompletePlanet link (under "Intelligent search agents"). A search form appears.

- In the Find databases relevant to text box, type "invisible Web" OR "deep Web" and then select the As a Boolean query option in the adjacent list box. Click the Go button. A list of the first 10 search results appears.

- Print the page and add your name to the top.

- Compare the first 10 search results from CompletePlanet with those from ProFusion that you gathered in Steps a–i above. Note that CompletePlanet found some different listings from ProFusion. Therefore, you conclude that using more than one intelligent search engine provides better coverage of the Web.

Now that you know how to search the invisible Web, you want to use an intelligent search agent to check the latest news and newsgroups on ice hockey leagues. Go to IncyWincy's home page from the Student Online Companion (located under "Intelligent search agents"), and drill down to the page shown in Figure D-19. Print a copy of the page and add your name at the top.

FIGURE D-19

News
tech biz health world

Meta Search
business jobs movies topical

International
brazil france germany

Web Search
arts business health world

The Invisible Web Search Engine

Page Options

Create Account
Personalize Search

[   ] [Search]

☑ Search only in National Hockey League ()

Top : Sports : Hockey : Ice Hockey : Leagues : **National Hockey League (1,927)**

Sites about the National Hockey League (NHL), NHL teams' official pages, fan pages, news and media, schedules, players and statistics.

Categories

Chats and Forums (7)   Magazines and E-zines@ (3)   Statistics (16)
Fan Pages (43)   News and Media (26)   **Teams** (823)
Fantasy@ (91)   Organizations (1)
History (27)   **Players** (983)

Sites

NHL.com · cached · The official National Hockey League web site includes features, news, rosters, statistics, schedules, teams, live game radio broadcasts, and video clips.

Glossary

Algorithm A mathematical formula used by a search engine to rank each Web site returned in search results according to the terms used in the search query.

AND Boolean operator that connects keywords in a search query. AND narrows a search and decreases the number of search results because each word connected with AND must be on a Web page for it to be included in the results. Every additional keyword connected to a search by AND further narrows the search. Most search tools use AND as the default Boolean operator, whether you enter it or not. Many search tools accept the plus sign (+) to indicate AND. Some search tools may require AND or the plus sign if the tool defaults to the OR operator. *See also* Boolean operator.

AND NOT Boolean operator that connects keywords in a search query. Using AND NOT narrows a search and decreases the number of search results because each word must not be on a Web page for it to be included in the results. Every additional keyword connected to a search by AND NOT further narrows the search. Most search tools require the use of the minus sign (-) to indicate AND NOT. *See also* Boolean operator.

Annotation Summary or review of a Web page, usually written by experts, such as professionals, academics in the field, or librarians.

Bookmarks A function of the Netscape browser that allows for easy storage, organization, and revisiting of Web pages. This browser feature is called Favorites in Internet Explorer.

Boolean logic A logic system, based on simple algebra and developed by mathematician George Boole, which defines how Boolean operators manipulate sets of data. Also known as Boolean algebra. It is represented graphically with Venn diagrams.

Boolean operators Command words such as AND, OR, and AND NOT that narrow, expand, or restrict a search based on Boolean logic.

Cached page Copy of a Web page that resides on a search engine's computer.

Citation format A style guide that standardizes references to resources like books, magazine articles, and Web pages. Common formats are those by MLA (Modern Language Association) and APA (American Psychological Association).

Complex query A search query that uses Boolean operators to define the relationships between keywords and phrases in a way that search tools can interpret.

Corporate author A committee, association, or group credited with creating a work such as a Web page.

Deep Web *See* Invisible Web.

Default operator The Boolean operator that a search engine automatically uses in a query, whether typed as part of the query or not. Most search engines default to the AND operator, although a few default to the OR operator.

Dewey Decimal system A numeric subject classification system used in many libraries. Named after its inventor Melville Dewey.

Discussion group *See* Newsgroup.

Directory *See* Subject guide.

Distributed subject guide Subject guide created by a variety of editors working somewhat independently and usually stored on numerous computers around the country or the world. Like a regular subject guide, it hierarchically arranges links to Web pages based on topics and sub-topics. Though many distributed subject guides are excellent, they often lack standardization and can be uneven in quality.

Domain The last two or three letters of a URL. URLs from the U.S. typically end in three letters, indicating the type of site, such as *.gov*, *.edu*, *.org*, or *.com*. URLs from other countries typically end in two letters, indicating the country of origin, such as *.ca* (*Canada*), *.uk* (*United Kingdom*), or *.jp* (*Japan*).

Drilling down Clicking through subject headings (or topics or categories) to reach relevant links. Typically the subject topics are arranged from the more general to the more specific.

Dynamically generated Web pages Pages generated by a database in response to a specific query. One kind of page found in the invisible Web.

Evaluative criteria Standards used to determine if a Web site is appropriate for your needs. These standards usually include considerations of organization, authority, objectivity, accuracy, scope, and currency.

Favorites A function of the Internet Explorer browser that allows for easy storage, organization, and revisiting of Web pages. This browser feature is called Bookmarks in Netscape.

Filter *See* Search filter.

Forcing the order of operation Using parentheses in a complex query to force the search tool to look at the words inside the parentheses first, which can greatly affect search results. If not forced, search tools typically search keywords from left to right.

Forum *See* Newsgroup.

Hierarchy A ranked order. Hierarchies commonly used in Internet subject guides include topical, alphabetical, and geographical. Topical hierarchies typically go from the more general to the more specific.

HTML (Hypertext markup language) A coded format language used to create and control the appearance of documents on the Web. *See also* Web page.

Intelligent search agent A software program that automatically retrieves information stored on multiple databases and aids in accessing information on the invisible Web. Also called a search bot. Examples include ProFusion and IncyWincy.

Internet A vast global network of interconnected networks that allows you to find and connect to information on the Web.

Internet search tools Services which help locate information on the Web and the Internet, including search engines, metasearch engines, subject guides, specialized search tools, and intelligent search agents.

Intersection The place where two sets overlap in a Venn diagram. Results from the use of the Boolean AND.

Invisible Web The part of the Web inaccessible to search engine spiders. It consists of information housed in databases, as well as much of the Web's data in .pdf, .doc, and other non-HTML file formats. Also known as the deep Web. The invisible Web is many times, perhaps 500 times, larger than the visible Web. A small part of the invisible Web can be accessed with intelligent search agents.

Keyword An important word that describes a major concept of your search topic.

List address The mailing list address to which correspondence is sent. *See* also Subscription address.

Listserv A software program that supports interactive Internet communication, such as the use of mailing lists.

Mailing list A form of interactive Internet communication which allows e-mailing messages to all other members of a list automatically. Often called a Listserv after the software that supports it.

Metasearch engine A search tool that searches the indexes of multiple search engines simultaneously. Better metasearch engines, such as Ixquick and ProFusion, present your query to various search engines in the ways they will understand it. Since most do not, it is usually best to metasearch with only simple searches.

Minus sign Used by many search tools as a symbol for the Boolean AND NOT.

Mnemonic Assisting or aiding memory. For example, many URLs are mnemonic to make them easier to remember.

Netiquette The protocol and common rules of courtesy used by people on the Internet, particularly in discussion groups or newsgroups.

Newsgroup A form of interactive Internet communication which serves as a virtual bulletin board where messages on thousands of topics are posted daily. Often called a Usenet group after the software upon which it runs. Also called discussion groups and forums.

Or Boolean operator that connects keywords in a search query. Using OR broadens or expands a search and increases the number of search results because any of the words can be on a Web page for it to be included in the results. Every additional keyword connected to a search by OR further broadens the search. *See also* Boolean operator.

Order of operation *See* Forcing the order of operation.

Parentheses Used around two or more keywords combined with Boolean operators, parentheses force the order of operation of a search query by indicating that the part of the search inside the parentheses should be performed first.

Periodical database A specialized database that contains the full text of articles from periodicals, such as newspapers, magazines, and journals. Common periodical databases are ProQuest, InfoTrac, and EbscoHost. This kind of database usually requires a paid subscription and is only available at libraries.

Phrase searching Forcing the search tool to search only for pages containing a phrase, or two or more words together in a certain order. Typically quotation marks are used around the words to indicate that they should be searched as a phrase. Phrases can be used with Boolean operators in the same ways a keyword can be used.

Plus sign Used by many search tools as a symbol for the Boolean AND.

Portal A large Web gateway providing access to huge amounts of information. It often includes search engines, news, shopping, e-mail, chat, and more. A portal that focuses on one topic or industry is called a vertical portal or a vortal.

Query *See* Search query.

Quotation marks Used around two or more keywords in a search form, quotation marks indicate to most search tools that the words should be searched as a phrase.

Scope The range of topics covered by a Web site. The scope of a site may be narrow, covering a smaller range of topics, or broad, covering a wider range of topics.

Search bot *See* Intelligent search agent.

Search engine A search tool, usually indexed by spiders, that locates Web pages containing the keywords entered in a search form.

Search filter A program used by search tools, usually from Advanced Search pages, to specifically include or exclude Web pages according to criteria such as language, file format, date, and domain. Whenever a filter is used, results are limited. Every additional filter used in a search further limits the results.

Search form The place where a user enters a search query at a search tool. It can be one text box or a complex array of text boxes, filters, and drop-down menus.

Search query Keywords, phrases, and/or Boolean operators entered into a search form that the search tool uses to search its index.

Set The term used for a group in Boolean logic. In a Venn diagram a set is commonly represented as a circle.

Site map An index to the pages on a Web site.

Specialized search tool A Web site that provides access to data stored in online databases that require direct access, making traditional search engines and most subject guides ineffective. Specialized search tools include online telephone directories, reference tools, online maps, and online periodicals.

Specialized search engine A search engine that limits the Web pages it indexes by subject. A specialized search engine often combines the power of Boolean searching with the focus of a subject guide.

Spider A computer program that scans, or crawls, the Web to index Web pages. The spider-created index is searched when you query a search engine. Spiders do not make judgments regarding the value of indexing a page as human indexers do.

Stop words Common words, such as *a, and, the, for,* and *of* that are not normally searched by search tools.

Subject directory *See* Subject guide.

Subject guide A search tool that hierarchically arranges links to Web pages. The links are evaluated and annotated by people, usually subject specialists or librarians, as opposed to spiders. Also called subject directory, subject index, or subject tree.

Subject index *See* Subject guide.

Subject tree *See* Subject guide.

Subscription Payment made to the owner or distributor of digital information for online access for a specified period of time, usually a year.

Subscription address A mailing list address to which messages requesting e–mail addresses be added or dropped from a list are sent. Also known as the administrative address. *See also* List address.

Synonyms Words that have similar meanings. In an online search, synonyms are normally used to expand a search. They are usually connected by the Boolean operator OR.

Syntax Rules of a language, like grammar, that standardize usage. In computer searching, syntax governs the form queries must take to instruct a search tool to perform a certain function.

Thread A sub-topic of newsgroup postings. A discussion starts with one posting. Subsequent postings in response to it, no matter how many there are, are considered one thread.

Trailblazer page A Web page that links to numerous sites covering all aspects of a topic. Often trailblazer pages are compiled by experts in a field.

Union The combination of two sets in a Venn diagram. Results from use of the Boolean OR.

Usenet *See* Newsgroup.

Venn diagrams Drawings, typically comprised of interacting circles, used to illustrate Boolean logic or searches using Boolean operators. First developed by mathematician John Venn.

Visible Web The portion of the Web that is indexed by search engine spiders. Also may refer to parts of the Web that, while not crawled by spiders, are indexed by subject guides. The visible Web is many times, perhaps 500 times, smaller than the invisible Web.

Vortal A vertical portal. *See also* Portal.

Web *See* World Wide Web.

Web page The most common type of document on the World Wide Web. Most results from search engines and subject guides are Web pages, which are usually written in hypertext markup language, or HTML, and have file extensions of .htm or .html. Other types of file formats include .pdf (Adobe Acrobat), .ppt (PowerPoint), .xls (Excel), and .doc (WORD). These non-HTML documents are more likely to be part of the invisible Web and best accessed with intelligent search agents.

Web site Stores, links, and delivers Web pages. A Web site can range in size from one Web page to thousands of Web pages.

World Wide Web An enormous repository of information stored on millions of computers all over the world.

Index